Swin, Swale & Swatchway

The Teal Ashore

SWIN, SWALE
& SWATCHWAY

or

Cruises down the Thames,
The Medway and the Essex Rivers

by

H. LEWIS JONES, M.A.

assisted by

C. B. LOCKWOOD

Lodestar Books

First published 1892 by Waterlow and Sons Limited, London
This edition published 2014 by
Lodestar Books
71 Boveney Road, London, SE23 3NL, United Kingdom

www.lodestarbooks.com

A CIP catalogue record for this book
is available from the British Library

ISBN 978-1-907206-30-6

Typeset by Lodestar Books in Equity

Printed in Spain by Graphy Cems, Navarra

All papers used by Lodestar Books
are sourced responsibly

CONTENTS

LIST OF ILLUSTRATIONS

PREFACE

THIS LITTLE BOOK HAS BEEN PUT TOGETHER from recollections of various cruises in and about the Thames Estuary, most of them in the little *Teal* of 3½ tons, with my partner, Mr. C. B. Lockwood, who has contributed many of the "yarns" herein related, who led the way as pilot in many of the more distant trips, and whose help in the collection of materials for the book I take this opportunity of acknowledging. Dr. C. E. Shelly has also been so good as to assist by writing a Chapter on the River Deben and Woodbridge.

The amusement which our voyages have afforded to our friends as well as to ourselves, and the pleasure with which we recall all the incidents of our early experiences afloat, have led to the composition of this short record of our adventures.

I am indebted to the kindness of the Editor of the *National Observer* for the reference to Dr. Jessop's *Lives of the Norths* which is given in Chapter I.

The illustrations are from photographs taken on the cruises. With three exceptions they were all done with the very convenient "Eclipse" Hand Camera made by Mr. Shew, of Newman Street, Oxford Street.

H. LEWIS JONES.
UPPER WIMPOLE STREET, W.

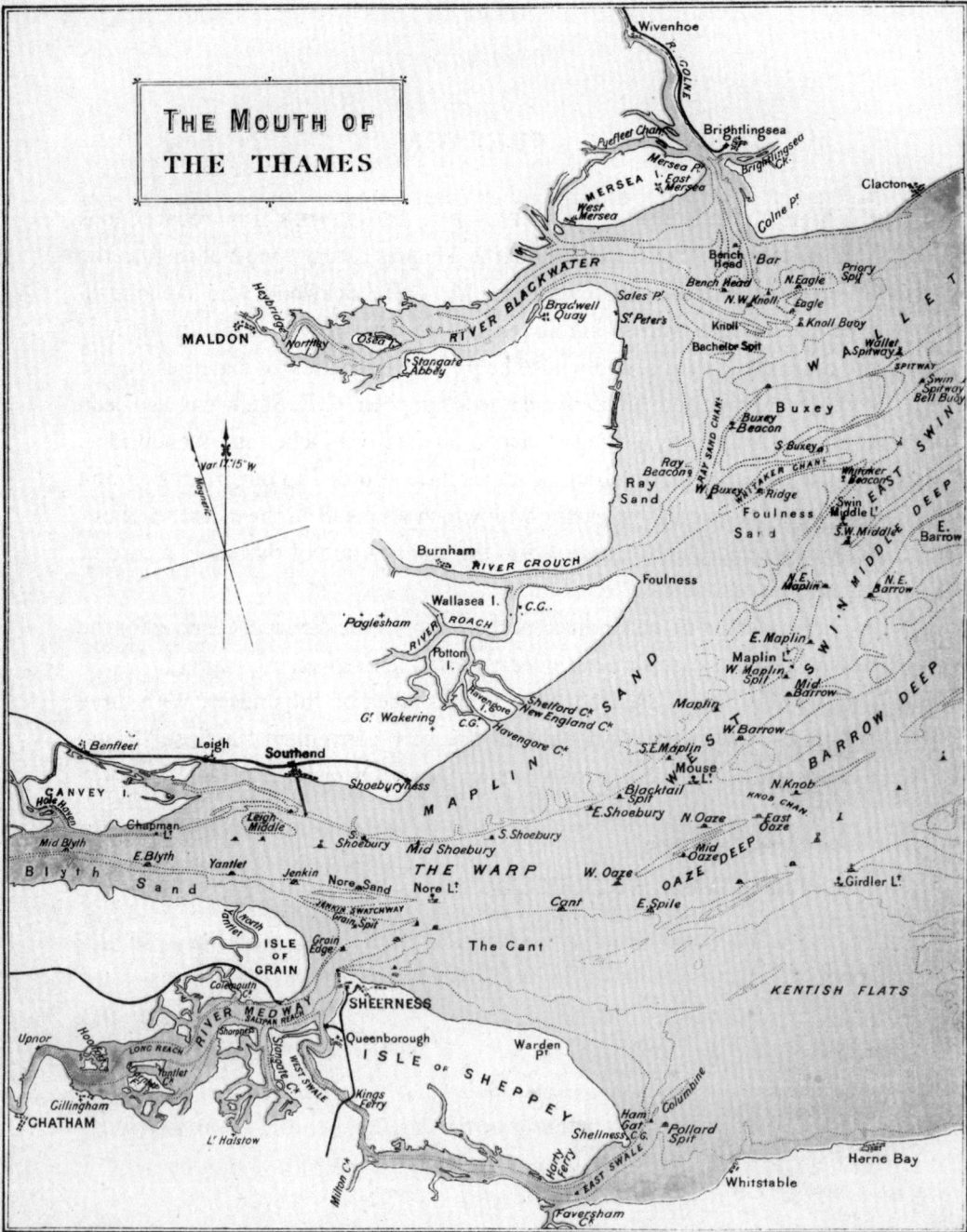

THE MOUTH OF THE THAMES

Wivenhoe

R. COLNE

Brightlingsea

Brightlingsea Ck.

Pyefleet Chan.

Mersea P.
E. Mersea
MERSEA I.
West Mersea

Clacton

Colne P.

Bench Head
Bench Head

Bar

N. Eagle

Priory Spit

N.W. Knoll

Eagle

Knoll

Knoll Buoy

Wallet

Sales P.

St. Peter's

Bradwell Quay

RIVER BLACKWATER

Hybridge

Osea I.

Northey

MALDON

Stangate Abbey

Bachelor Spit

W. Spitway

SPITWAY

Swin Spitway
Bell Buoy

WALLET

Buxey

Buxey Beacon

S. Buxey

W. Buxey

Ridge

Whitaker Beacon

Swin Middle L.

S.W. Middle

E. Barrow

Var 11°15' W.

Magnetic

Ray Beacons

W. Buxey

WHITAKER CHAN.

Foulness Sard

N.E. Maplin

N.E. Barrow

Ray Sand

RAY SAND CHAN.

EAST SWIN

SWIN MIDDLE DEEP

Burnham

RIVER CROUCH

Foulness

Wallasea I.

RIVER ROACH

C.G.

Paglesham

Potton I.

Shelford C.

New England C.

E. Maplin

Maplin L.
W. Maplin Spit

Mid. Barrow

BARROW DEEP

G. Wakering

Havengore

C.G.

Havengore C.

Maplin

W. Barrow

WEST SWIN

MAPLIN SAND

S.E. Maplin

Benfleet

Leigh

Southend

Mouse L.

N. Knob

KNOB CHAN.

Shoeburyness

Blacktail Spit

S.E. Maplin

N. Knob

CANVEY I.

Hole Haven

Chapman

Leigh Middle

Shoebury

S. Shoebury

Mid Shoebury

S. Shoebury

E. Shoebury

N. Oaze

East Oaze

Mid Blyth

E. Blyth

Yantlet

Jenkin

Nore Sand

THE WARP

W. Oaze

Mid Oaze

OAZE DEEP

Blyth Sand

Nore L.

Cant

E. Spile

Girdler L.

ISLE OF GRAIN

Yantlet

North

KNOB SWATCHWAY

Grain Spit

Grain Edge

The Cant

KENTISH FLATS

Upnor

Colemouth

Hoo

RIVER MEDWAY

SALTPAN REACH

SHEERNESS

LONG REACH

Yantlet C.

Sharpness

Queenborough

Warden P.

Gillingham

WEST SWALE

STANGATE CK.

Kings Ferry

ISLE of SHEPPEY

Columbine

CHATHAM

L. Halstow

Horty Ferry

Ham Gat
Shellness C.G.

Pollard Spit

Milton C.

EAST SWALE

Whitstable

Herne Bay

Faversham

CHAPTER I

Introductory

SWITZERLAND IS OFTEN CALLED THE PLAYGROUND of Europe, and of those who crowd thither every summer for their holiday not a few are dwellers in our modern Babylon; but there is another glorious playground close at home for Londoners which is not nearly so much used nor so well known as it deserves, and that is the lower Thames, from Gravesend to the Nore, with the Medway and its numerous creeks, the Swale, and those almost unknown Essex rivers, the Crouch, the Roach and the Blackwater, which in their tidal reaches offer such a fine sailing ground for small craft, as the few who have explored them very well know. The upper Thames is all very well in its way, with its houseboats, water-parties, gaudy-coloured blazers, banjo-accompaniments, and such soft delights, but it is all tame when compared with the stirring incidents of salt-water sailing; and those bolder spirits who can enjoy roughing it do find in and about Sea Reach an endless variety of adventure and of mimic hardship, and breezes ten times more invigorating than any to be had in the Thames valley.

At the Thames mouth the jaded Londoner can, if he pleases, spend his Saturday to Monday in a new world, breathing a keen sea-air, and can fancy himself another Columbus as he anchors for the night in some lonely creek in an angle of the world well-nigh inaccessible except in a small boat, and, if the thought gives him any satisfaction, he can feel, as the Major-General's daughters did in the *Pirates of Penzance*, that he is in a spot where human foot has never trod before. Snugly berthed in the little two or three tonner, which he has learnt to trust, and which he knows will take him safe home when the time comes to catch his last train for London, he can serenely contemplate the sunset through a grateful cloud of tobacco smoke, and think cheerfully of his prospects on the morrow, even if he foresee a dusting while turning the little vessel to windward for home twenty or thirty miles away.

There are many men who love Sea Reach with that true love of salt water which is to be found lurking somewhere in the hearts of most Englishmen, and all through the summer these noble sportsmen are to be met with, spending their week ends on their little yachts, and picking up health and hardening their fibre for that struggle for existence which grows more and more deadly every year; but their numbers are as naught compared with those who might become good sailor-men if only they knew how to take the first step, and could be made aware of the fun to be had in pottering about in those nooks and corners of the Kent and Essex shores which are to be found by those who care to look for them; but, alas, it must be confessed that too often the yachtsman's ideas seem unable to soar above the same old cruises to Chatham or to Queenborough, to Hole Haven or to Ramsgate, as though to do these were to exhaust the resources of the Thames mouth. And then, again, there is that mysterious desire to go ashore which seems to come on after a man has been a few hours in a boat, which compels him to forsake his vessel as soon as ever his anchor is down and his sails stowed, in order that he may go and loaf on shore. This feeling naturally drives him to the seaports and towns, and stands in the way of that full knowledge of the rivers which is learnt by those who can enjoy the solitude of an anchorage "far from the madding crowd." Perhaps, after all, this is the fault of some old Viking instinct in the blood, which sees in each town some prospect of plunder or "divarsion"! and additional support to this view is to be found in the manner in which these descents upon the coast are performed; for when your boat sailor has made his passage, regardless of appearances, he will go ashore in all the pride of his old jersey, sea-coat and thigh boots, carrying possibly the ship's bucket in his hand to carry off his plunder in. He seems to regard the town, or highly respectable cathedral city, no more than if it were a desert island, the shops are merely convenient stores of the needful victuals for the cruise, and what the natives think of him is as nothing in his eyes. I have known men who at home are most particular about their dress and appearance in public, to go about a town (that is, if they have reached it by small boat) in an old flannel shirt, open at the neck, and with no collar, or wearing sea-boots and a Cardigan jacket (which is like to level all ranks by making everyone look like a cabin steward), and in this garb to make their purchases. I have heard of a man, a Master of Arts, or an LL.D., or something of that kind, who went into South-end thus attired to buy strawberries, taking the boat's bucket along to carry them in, and he was such a sight that an indignant native on the pier couldn't help asking him if he thought they were all savages there, that he went about in such a disreputable style; and when he called for letters at the post office, the good and kind postmistress handed him a post-card, saying, "Shall I read it to you, my man?"

It is true that collars do not keep well if kicked about a small boat, or stowed under the mattress for a day or two at a time; and it is also very diffi-cult, according to Charles Kingsley, for anyone to look like a gentleman when he has no collar on; but one way out of the difficulty is to wear a blue jersey with a high neck to it, for this provides at least a kind of covering or collar for the throat, and looks better than a muffler, the latter being at least a little out of place on a broiling hot day.

I should like to see an essay written by some learned professor of moral science upon the peculiar state of mind which is produced by living much at sea. That there is such a peculiarity is acknowledged by the manners and customs which we recognise as the attributes of the stage sailor, and most of us have had opportunities of recognising their free and independent spirit, be they men-of-war's men, enjoying a day's leave on shore, and knocking one another down for the pure fun of the thing, or be they merchant-men or fish-ermen, but especially does it show itself among fishermen, whose tendencies can develop uncontrolled by the strict discipline which is found on big ships.

Fishermen everywhere assume to themselves as a matter of course a su-periority over the landsmen of their own neighbourhood, whom they some-what contemptuously call "countrymen;" and, in addition to the smartness and self-reliance which is brought out by the risks and chances of their call-ing, they seem to preserve a large amount of the old predatory instinct, due perhaps to the fact that they hunt for their daily bread in a more primitive and direct way than most other folks; possibly, too, there is something in their temporary escape from police and other supervision while at sea which may at times seduce them into a belief that force is a sufficient remedy, and that everybody must protect himself or go to the wall. Once when cross-tacking, in company with another little boat, I asked the fisherman who was with us whether he meant to stand on or to give way, and his reply was significant enough: "We are bigger than what they are—we may as well stand on." Nevertheless I think that sailors, and fishermen, and bargemen, look with a kindly eye upon the amateur boat sailor, who is their swallow, the harbinger of summer weather, and no more a competitor of theirs in the struggle for existence than the swallow is of the sea-gull, and they are generally ready enough to give way to a small boat when she and they are working to windward together, provided, of course, that the little one be on the starboard tack. We have always made it a rule in meeting another vessel to let them see what we mean to do. If a boat means to bear away, let her do so in good time; or if she means to luff up and stand on, let her make it plain from the first. Nothing is more annoying than to see an approaching boat bear up one minute and come to the next, as though not knowing her own mind.

It has been our good fortune to sail a boat for the past five years, part of the time about Chatham and the Medway in a little two-ton cutter, *The Wild Rose*, and afterwards in the *Teal*, a four tonner, yawl-rigged, in Sea Reach and round about the Thames Estuary, and we have been surprised that men do not seem to know or care about knowing the creeks and anchorages in out-of-the-way spots. One rarely sees little vessels except in a few of the best known places. How many of the owners of small craft, I would ask, know the ins and outs of Colemouth Creek, of Stangate, or the Yantlet to the south of Long Reach in the Medway, or can get in or out of Havengore Creek, or have been to Paglesham or Mersea Island, all these places being retreats, at once picturesque, novel and delightful? When questioned, they have heard of them, but have never been there; or say they would like to go if they knew the channel, and were not afraid of getting stuck up on shore.

Nowadays, improvements in hull and rig make it possible to put to sea safely in smaller and less costly craft than formerly, and many of the keenest members of the yachting world are to be found among the men who can enjoy the mimic (?) hardships of a little eighteen or twenty foot boat, and can feel at home in the short seas and yeasty popple generally found about the Nore.

Give us the man who can greet with laughter the spray as it comes smashing aft over the weather bow, and thinks it a good joke to find his sea-boots full of water, which has reached them down the back of his neck, and can think of the well-earned pipe of peace which he will enjoy when he has found his way into some little harbour, and has changed his wet things and is demolishing his supper in comfort. He will chuckle when he thinks of the time when he had to be content, from lack of knowledge, to spend the night anchored outside rolling heavily, as one may see little craft roll many a time off Southend Pier, off Port Victoria, or on the edge of the Bligh Sand.

To our minds, there is nothing more conducive to mental repose than the sight of a harbour or navigable river with its ever-changing views of coasters, barges and other small craft, each one a study in itself; and we know a man eminent in his profession who is satisfied that no one can tread the "serener heights" of surgery unless he sails a small boat, and he says that he has often left London feeling as cross as a lady post-office clerk, but that after loitering an hour by the waterside at Gravesend, Sheerness or Chatham, he finds himself calming down, so that a child might play with him.

Fielding, in the account of his *Voyage to Lisbon*, seems to have felt this influence of the Thames and shipping, for he breaks out into philosophical reflections on the subject, as for instance—"I cannot pass by another observation on the deplorable want of taste in our enjoyments, which we show by almost totally neglecting the pursuit of what seems to me the highest degree of amusement, this is the sailing ourselves in little vessels of our own, contrived only for our ease and accommodation ... This amusement I confess, if enjoyed in any perfection, would be of the expensive kind; but such expense would not exceed the reach of a moderate fortune, and would fall very short of the prices which are daily paid for pleasures of a far inferior rate. The truth, I believe, is that sailing in the manner I have just mentioned is a pleasure rather unknown or unthought of than rejected by those who have experienced it." Then in another place he says: "For my own part I confess myself so entirely fond of a sea prospect that

I think nothing on land can equal it; and, if it be set off with shipping, I desire to borrow no ornament from the terra firma." And he describes the pleasure he enjoyed "in viewing a succession of ships with all their sails expanded to the winds bounding over the waves before us." See, too, in the book, which can now be bought for sixpence, the amusing story of a collision with a cod-smack at Gravesend, and the observations of the shrewd old Bow Street police magistrate upon the manners and customs of sailors and waterside folk.[1]

The Hon. Roger North (time 1685) has a very interesting account of his little yacht, which he kept in London, and used for making passages down Swin, and so forth. He says: "I was extremely fond of being master of anything that would sail; and Mr. John Windham encouraged me with a present of a yacht, which I kept four years on the Thames, and received great delight in her. This yacht was small, but had a cabin and a bedroom athwart ships aft the mast and a large locker at the helm; the cookroom, with a cabin for a servant, was forward on, with a small chimney at the very prow. Her ordinary sail was a boom mainsail, a stay foresail and a jib; all wrought aft, so we could sail without a hand ahead, which was very troublesome because of the spray that was not (sailing to windward) to be endured. She was no good sea-boat, because she was open aft, and might ship a sea to sink her, especially before the wind in a storm, but in the river she would sail tolerably and work extraordinarily well. She was ballasted with cast lead. It was a constant entertainment to sail against smacks and hoys, of which the river was always full. At stretch they were too hard for me, but by I had the better, for I commonly did in two what they could scarce get in three boards."

He further tells us that when he went for a long trip he laid in cold meats in tin cases, bottles of beer, ale, and for the seamen brandy, adding, "and though our meat was coarse (beef for the most part), yet no epicure enjoyed it so much as we did."

With a good gale they "got down in one tide as low as the Ooze Edge, where is a buoy," and there lay for the next tide. "In the evening the wind slackened and the surge yet wrought, which was a most uneasy condition

---

1 Fielding, *A Voyage to Lisbon*, Cassell's National Library.

to lie, stamping and tossing without a breath of wind to pay our sail, which flapped about most uneasily. There was wind aloft, though I was too humble to enjoy it, for empty colliers came down with topsails out, full bunted, and bows rustling, which did not a little provoke me; but patience is a seaman's capital and necessary virtue." Next morning they weighed anchor and proceeded, and with a fresh wind stemmed the tide, and, "it being high water at the spits, we ran over all past the Gunfleet" and reached Harwich.

"There was little remarkable," he informs us, in this day's voyage, "only that I, with my friend Mr. Chute, sat before the mast in the hatchway, with prospectives and books, the magazine of provisions, and a boy to make a fire and help broil, make tea, chocolate, etc.; and thus, passing alternately from one entertainment to another, we sat out eight whole hours and scarce knew what time was past. For the day proved cool, the gale brisk, air clear and no inconvenience to molest us, nor wants to trouble our thoughts, neither business to importune nor formalities to tease us, so that we came nearer to a perfection of life there than I was ever sensible of otherwise." Good old Roger North; what an example he sets for the "top practices in Chancery" of the present day. And the rest of his acts and of his cruise, and all that he did, must be sought for in his own autobiography; and very entertaining it is.[1]

His remarks are all as fresh and as suitable to the present time as though written yesterday, instead of over two hundred years ago. He comments upon the "ugly shelf at the point of the country between the Thames and Maldon waters," the Whitaker and Buxey, and says that there were several wrecks upon it. There are some now, and doubtless there have been others; keeping up a sort of apostolic succession of wrecks all through the two hundred years which have elapsed, and tells us that there is a great mast set down at the point which they call the Shoe Beacon. From an old map this seems to have stood about where the Maplin lighthouse now is.

In the early days of the *Teal* she possessed a petroleum stove for cooking, and for two years did her crew groan and suffer under that incubus. One of our friends declares that he never smells petroleum to this day without think-

---

1 Dr. Jessop, *The Lives of the Norths*, Geo. Bell and Sons.

ing of the *Teal*. It infected the whole boat, and, what is more, it took about an hour to boil the kettle over the thing. At last we revolted, threw it overboard, and tried another. But that soon followed the first one; and we bought a good and very powerful spirit apparatus. What a comfort the change was! How we ever endured the petroleum horror is a mystery!

The boat is a great source of amusement to some of our friends; and they never seem tired of asking us the same questions, the following being samples: "Do you sleep on board? What do you do at night; you don't sail all the time, I suppose? What do you do when you want to anchor? I suppose you take a man to sail the boat for you." Once I was asked by a friend, to whom I showed a photograph of a Thames barge, whether that was the ship I went to Australia in; and, on another occasion, a lady refused to take the slightest interest in a pretty picture of a yacht under sail, because it did not belong to anyone that she knew. The continual repetition of the same questions about the boat reminds one of the questions people invariably address to amateur photographers. "I suppose you use those new dry plates." (N.B. Ninety-nine amateurs out of a hundred have never seen any other sort, and it is rather a stretch of the imagination to call dry plates new in these days.) "Do you use the instantaneous process? Do you think they will ever be able to photograph in colours?" That is the regular broadside; and I ask my photographic friends how often they have been called upon to face it?

The first problem to be seriously considered is the kind of boat best suited for cruising at the mouth of the Thames. In the first place, those who have big vessels or small deep racing craft are shut out of a great deal of the amusement of exploring the creeks and odd corners of the river; to them it is a serious matter to get "ketched up on a bit of a spit," so they are not likely to look upon such a state of things as fun, nor to run even the smallest risk of it: not that it is at all necessary for the explorer of creeks to run aground whenever he goes for a cruise—please don't think that, critical reader. Although to be hard and fast ashore must not be thought to be a constant practice of ours, yet it is important that if such a contingency should arise, even once in a season, it is very different when the result is merely a certain degree of discomfort than when it is a matter of serious anxiety whether she will float again when the tide returns. We have been well brought up to "follow the sea" by the trusty Benson, and to use the lead line and the sounding pole in a proper manner, and when there is a passage to be made, or when the tide is ebbing, we can manage to keep clear of the points, for to lie aground on the mud for several hours at a time plays no part in the cruises of the *Teal*, though on a flowing tide and in fine weather we may sometimes allow ourselves to cut it a little fine round the tail of a spit.

The advantages of a three-foot draught are that the man with a slender purse can explore the vasty deeps (and shallows) of the Thames estuary and enjoy himself quite as much as his deep-keeled brethren, for he can go into the very places which they avoid like poison; and further, he picks up any amount of local knowledge of the river, from the careful study of the channels with chart and lead line, and soon grows into an accomplished mud pilot, able to take the boat clear through devious channels, and by so doing to cut off long stretches of turning to windward, and to save many a valuable half-hour when time is short.

Give us a boat drawing from three feet to three feet six, with six or seven feet beam, and twenty feet on the water line, strongly built, a full model and fairly high topsides; not too much keel, but what there is carried well fore and aft to hold her well up to windward in a rough sea, with a ton of lead ballast and a snug sail plan, yawl or cutter, the former for choice, because by stowing the mizen and putting on a smaller jib, the craft can be so rapidly snugged down for a stiff peck to windward, without the bother of reefing the mainsail, and because it is a real advantage to be able to sail under jib and mizen when proceeding with caution in unknown waters, or when about to bring up in a crowded harbour. Such a boat as this is big enough to stand a lot of weather, and is not too heavy to be helped round with an oar or shoved off should she get ashore even on a falling tide, if the crew go aft or forward as need be, to alter the vessel's trim. Once or twice, at critical times, our crew has even tumbled overboard *en masse* to help her off the sands.

The sail area a boat can safely carry depends so much upon the skill of her crew that they must be the best judges of what they are prepared to tackle,

merely bearing in mind that perpetual reefing is intolerable, and that in Sea
Reach and the Swin Channel there is usually as much wind as a twenty-foot
boat wants; and that after all the whole object of the business is to enjoy oneself and have the benefit of salt-water holidays, and not merely to go in for sailorising and thrashing her through it. The man who talks most of the delights
of heavy weather is usually the one who has not had much of it, for when he
has he is usually well able to appreciate the comfort of fine weather. Still a fast
boat is useful at times, but speed is not safe if it be got from over-sparring.

The decks and cabin top must be strong and good and water-tight, and
though too much of a cabin top looks lubberly, and rather spoils the smartness
of a craft, yet when a small boat has to serve a double purpose, namely, to be
first a boat, and secondly a floating house, one must have shelter and live with
some approach to comfort while away on the cruise, therefore cabin room and
good sleeping accommodation, dry and warm, are essential. No one can enjoy
small boat sailing unless he can keep himself warm and dry at night, so as to
sleep well and awake in the morning refreshed, and with a cheerful countenance, at any hour by the clock. Rain, spray and cold wind can be disregarded
by day if there is the certainty of a dry, warm cabin for the evening and night.

An useful part of one's outfit in these days is a camera, especially one of
the modern detective or hand cameras, for to snatch the visions of the fleeting
hours, and preserve them in the form of negatives for future use on winter
evenings with the magic lantern.

The actual size of a boat is less important than its handiness, as is well
seen in the way a Thames barge of eighty tons can be managed by its crew of
two men, and on a small boat everything should be planned with that object
steadily in view. The jib should traverse clear of the forestay, or, at any rate,
it should work without any need to go forward to clear it every time the boat
is in stays; and the jibsheets, too, should run freely without the necessity of
overhauling them; the working of a boat cannot be too easy; there are plenty
of opportunities for sailorising in the handiest of boats, and any extra labour,
however slight, soon becomes troublesome, and swallows up the energy
which can be better applied in making the passage.

Problem number two—What is the best place for a Londoner to make his head-quarters, and to keep his boat in? This is an awful problem. There is no best place, although there are several good ones, but each has some drawback. Either there is too much traffic, and a consequent risk of being run into at anchor, or there is no room for a comfortable berth, or there is a bad train service, or no one to take care of her when the owners are away, or she takes the ground for too long at low water. These are the chief difficulties, though not the only ones, and perfect head-quarters have yet to be discovered. Among the possible places are Erith, Purfleet, Greenhithe, Gravesend, Tilbury, Hole Haven, Leigh, Southend, Sheerness, Queenborough, Port Victoria, Upnor, Chatham, Rochester Bridge—all with some advantages and all with drawbacks.

We have kept our little vessel at Leigh for three or four seasons; and, although we grumble regularly in true British fashion at the disadvantages of the place, and constantly threaten that we will stand them no longer, but go elsewhere, yet we don't go. The place has good points as well as disadvantages, and these, helped by force of habit, have combined to keep us there year after year. All places where men keep their boats have some fault; so we prefer to bear the ills we have, and put up with the one great drawback to Leigh, namely, the lack of water.

The *Teal* floats at her mooring for about three hours each high water time, lying aground for the remainder of the tide; and this has to be met by suiting the time of departure to the tides, or by having the boat laid off in deep water, so that we can then row out or walk out over the mud in sea-boots to her on our arrival. All this, of course, is a nuisance; but, on the other hand, we have at Leigh a good and cheap train service, especially now that most fast trains for Southend stop at Leigh to take tickets. The boat lies close to the railway station. We have the most excellent of boat-keepers, with a convenient shed, and we are free from all risks of collision; and, as she dries out each tide, her bottom keeps free from weed. Moreover, there is no time lost in getting to sea, no journey up and down a horrible river swarming with steamers to use up half one's time before the open water of Sea Reach can be gained.

CHAPTER II
Leigh ~ The Ray ~ Benson

MY FIRST INTRODUCTION TO LEIGH and boat sailing was in 1880, when I went down there to have a first lesson in the art and mystery of the craft at the hands of my friend F., now far away in distant Vancouver, but still even there the possessor of a little vessel. F., a dear, good fellow, who had known the place for years, had the happy knack of getting on well with all the waterside folk, and delighted to know as many of the fishermen and inhabitants of the village as possible. He had gone through many phases of yachting; first, by the purchase and decking of an old ship's boat in St. Katharine's Docks at considerable cost, a well-known early stage of the yachting malady. They ballasted her with sand, in which were mussels; and these presently died, and made life on board intolerable; and she nearly foundered on her first voyage, by the bye. Then he became the proud possessor of a smart five tonner; and finally, at the time when I first knew him, he had settled down to take his weekly salting in a little sixteen-foot open boat, rigged with sprit sail and jib, and furnished with a heavy iron keel. In this he used to potter about over the tide and teach his friends the art and mystery of sailing, to hand, reef and steer, and "never for to quail at the fury of the gale," and all the use of head sail and after sail, and how to luff a little boat to the waves in a popple. Well do I remember his oft-repeated cry, sounding like an incantation at the shrine of Neptune, calling on the learner to keep her full, keep her full, till he had sufficiently impressed upon him the solemn importance of that cardinal principle; and, indeed, if yachts could speak, many of them, like him, would echo the same cry. The beginner never will keep his sails full when on a wind, but sags along with lifting jibs and slivering mainsail crab-like to leeward.

A glance at a map shows where Leigh stands, on the sunny slope of a hill at the head of a bight formed by the line of Essex coast and the eastern shore of Canvey Island, where the estuary of the Thames abruptly widens out from two miles to four miles in breadth, with a stretch of sands and mud dry at low water, reaching along the north shore of the river as far as Southend. The view of Leigh from the water is very picturesque, a foreground of fishing bawleys, a line of straggling cottages along Leigh Creek, backed by others rising in tiers irregularly one above the other, with bright red-tiled roofs and green trees and gardens, and the church at the top of the hill, and near to it a grove of elms where the rooks build and clamour all through the spring and early summer.

Leigh is reached by the London, Tilbury and Southend Railway from Fenchurch Street, and is the station next before Southend; the journey by the ordinary trains takes eighty minutes, but now most of the fast trains stop there, shortening the time by twenty minutes. The inhabitants of Leigh are nearly all fishermen, and their vessels, which are called bawleys, are cutters of about twenty tons, drawing six feet of water, clinker built, and with mainsails of great hoist, with long gaffs and no booms. There are over a hundred of these craft, and they make a brave show in Sea Reach, as they trawl under topsail, foresail and brailed mainsail. It is a very pretty sight to see them starting off in the grey of the morning, or coming home in the afternoon with their shrimps boiling, or being packed all ready for market. They chiefly trawl for shrimps, but also go whitebaiting, with spratting and long lining for cod in the winter time.

In the summer many of them go to Harwich, as the fishing there is better, and a jolly trip it is to go round in a bawley with them; they usually leave Leigh in May and return in September. Times are not nearly so good nowadays for them as they were, and the Leigh men feel it a good deal, for they have very serious competitors in the Dutch, who supply London from their sandbanks with any amount of shrimps, and cut down the prices of the Leigh shrimps all to nothing. The Dutchmen, too, have advantages in the way of through railway rates, which the Leigh men complain of bitterly.

Moreover, the Thames, whether from excessive fishing, or from the great amount of traffic, does not yield the harvest of the sea so plentifully as was the case fifty years ago, in spite of Sir J. B. Lawes' belief that the London sewage all turns into good fishes when it reaches the sea. For instance, in former days, the Leigh men used often to bring home turbot from off the Nore, but never now does that wily fish venture into those parts.

The bawleys lie at anchor in the Ray, and from a distance seem to form a regular forest of masts all along the channel. Here they lie afloat at all tides, and the fishermen go to and from them in their punts or foot-boats, over the flats or down Leigh Creek. Often as they come up the creek with the first of the flood the boats crowd along in a densely packed mass, now sticking fast aground and now floating on again as the tide rises, each boat with its two or three hampers of shrimps packed and labelled in readiness for the train. They boil their shrimps while under weigh, each vessel carrying a copper for the purpose; and the shrimps as soon as caught are cast into a seething cauldron of strong brine—salt water, with lumps of salt dissolved in it. This makes the shrimp dry and crisp, and imparts that special salt flavour which makes him harmonise so well with tea and watercresses, at ninepence a head.

A glance at the chart shows that Leigh stands at the head of a bay on a little creek which runs into Hadleigh Ray, or The Ray, about midway between Leigh and Southend. Leigh creek meanders through the wide mud flats which lie between the village and the Ray; while beyond the Ray is clean, hard sand off the end of Canvey Island, and beyond that again is Leigh Middle and the main channel. At high tide the flats are covered by about six feet of water, right up to their highest part opposite Leigh. Leigh Creek itself is bank full or "cant high" at two hours' flood. The old men in the village say that formerly there was much more water in the creek than there is now, and that their bawleys could lie always afloat about half way down it, but now the creek dries out to its junction with the Ray.

Recently the lower part of the Ray itself has been silting up fast, owing, it is said, to the mussels which were laid down on the edge of it a few years ago; also, no doubt, in part to the fact that a new channel, the Low Way, has opened out in the last few years across the outer sand, so that much of the water runs away through it, leaving too little to scour out the lower part of the Hadleigh Ray, called Leigh Swatch.

The whole place has an air of being silted up, and it is very probable that in a few more generations Leigh will find herself altogether high and dry, and her inhabitants will have to migrate elsewhere, or take to farming.

One of the oldest and, from our point of view, the chief inhabitant of Leigh is a retired fisherman, named Henry Cotgrove, a cheerful old man of close on seventy years, who devotes his energies to the care-taking of two or three little yachts, and also earns many an honest penny by taking visitors out for a row or a sail in the summer time. He is as keen and handy in a small boat as ever he was, and he knows every creek and sand-bank and set of tide within thirty miles and more. He is universally acknowledged to be the best boat sailor in Leigh; and many of the present generation of Leigh men have learnt their craft on his bawleys, and he boasts that he has made good fishermen of all he has had the training of. There are a good many Cotgroves in Leigh; and Henry Cotgrove often goes by the name of "Benson," because, as the story goes, when he was a boy, and used to go up to Billingsgate with fish in his father's bawley, before the railway was made, he won the heart of an apple-woman who had a stall near the market, and somehow her name has clung to him ever since, though the old lady is probably dead and buried these fifty years past. Benson has been shipkeeper to the *Teal* for five years; and many a yarn has he spun to us of the days of his youth, when shrimps fetched a good price and steamers were few, and collier brigs plenty, to bring the good sea-coal to London. There were good moneys to be made, too, by assisting them off the sands in bad weather; and even in fine weather they used to come up the river in such fleets that they would crowd each other ashore when tacking in company.

Many an aphorism has he fired off at us to sink deep into our memories, for "though he can't read, he knows more than many of them as can." He used to say to us, "A little boat will stand a deal of weather, if you have the heart to put her to it." "If you're sailing past a vessel that has taken the ground, remember her anchor is somewhere ahead of her, and may strike you." "If you ain't quite sure of your water, just you put your pole over and see what you've got." His friends used to say, "Them gents o' yours, Benson, will drownd theirselves one of these days;" but he would reply, "No; I don't think; they knows how to act within a little; they've got a stubborn little boat, and, if they do get into difficulties, it'll be their own fault." Yet when the *Teal* is away he generally keeps a sharp look out until he spies her in the offing, and on her return he can give a wonderfully good guess as to where she has been.

Leigh is not at all a bad place for head-quarters, provided always that one's boat does not draw more than about three feet of water. The station is close to the water's edge, which simplifies the labour of carrying one's stores and kit to and from the boat. What a business it is, staggering along with bags and rugs and things, both hands full and a parcel under each arm! and it is ten to one that something, generally a loaf of bread, topples out, which necessitates a full stop, to deposit one's whole cargo on the ground, to pick up the errant something, and then to re-stow cargo and take a fresh departure. There are some fair grocers' shops in Leigh, and a convenient inn, "The Ship", in which to change one's togs. "The Ship" folks, too, are always ready to send things down to the boat, and to replenish the boat's cellar for us with their best brand of ginger beer, the finest of drinks to take away on a cruise. The 'Pardner' has christened it Brut imperial, so Brut imperial is now with us its registered name, and no other is genuine.

The boat lies at a mooring a little way below the Coast Guard watch-house, where it was laid down for her by Benson when she first came to Leigh; and her bedding, kit-bags, oilskins, sea-boots, and such-like things are stored in Benson's shed close by. There is no particular difficulty in getting permission to lay down a mooring, but leave must be obtained before doing so; and she lies snugly on her mud bank under the eye of the Coast Guard, and there are none of those abominable light-fingered long-shoremen, who are not unknown at some other towns on the Thames and Medway. A friend of ours left his little boat for an hour on the beach at Southend, some years ago, while he went up into the town, and when he came back his mainsail was gone, having been cut away and stolen during his absence: even the sacred feeling about stealing a vessel's necessary gear being dead among the loafers of those parts.

The Coastguard Station, Leigh

One advantage gained by a boat which lies dry for several hours each tide is, that she keeps clean and free from weed very much longer than if she lies afloat all the time. Chatham river, in particular, is a dreadful place for the growth of weed. Then, in the winter, there are plenty of little sheltered creeks just above the village, for laying up craft, in which the boat just floats at the top of high water, and can easily be visited from time to time to be baled out and have her cabin aired. All these advantages would make the place a paradise, so now for the drawbacks. First, there is no water at Leigh during a large part of each tide. If one draws three feet, then there are two hours, or perhaps three, during which there is water over all up to the moorings, and at high water there are six feet of water right up to the shore; but when the tide has gone, there is no getting away for eight hours or so.

This want of water has to be made the best of by the Leigh people, and it is done in the following way: by choosing the time of starting so as to get clear away into deep water before nightfall—which is the plan for mid-day tides, or by getting away into the Ray, one mile off, and anchoring there for the night, and making a start in the morning; this is the plan for evening tides: or again, the boat can be anchored in the Ray before one's arrival, with a boy on board to put one off in the dinghy after walking over the flats to the edge of the Ray in sea-boots.

On returning from a cruise, similar tactics can be adopted, either sail in to moorings at high water, or leave her anchored in the Ray, to be fetched in afterwards, and walk ashore or paddle up Leigh Creek in the Berthon dinghy. There is water in Leigh Creek after an hour's flood for a Berthon boat.

The *Teal*'s crew very frequently sleep out in the Ray on their return from a cruise, and come in early in the morning in time for a breakfast on shore before the first train at 7.40 a.m. When there is water over all this is easy enough, and very delightful too it is in the grey of the early morning, just at daybreak, to come sliding in to the mooring like a phantom ship, when all is quiet on shore except the larks and nightingales. It is nearly always fine about sunrise, and the freshness of the air fully makes up for any short allowance of sleep.

On the morning before the Jubilee Yacht Race round England, the *Teal*, crew, passenger and ship's dog came into Leigh about four a.m. We had been becalmed the evening before, and about seven p.m., the ebb beginning to make down strong, we had anchored inside the West Shoebury buoy and turned in to sleep. We did not think much of the berth as a place to get a quiet night's rest in, because, what with the wash of steamers and the ripple produced by a breeze which sprung up about midnight, we rolled and sheered about a good deal; therefore, at three, leaving the passenger slumbering in his bunk, and making the ship's dog fast to the mizen with a rope's end, we pulled up hook and made for home. It was a fresh June morning, and the dawn was breaking behind us over the trees at Shoeburyness as we came round Southend Pier-head, threading our way through a fleet of beautiful yachts, collected together in readiness for the race; big racers and cruisers, rolling lazily to their anchors in the swell, with not a soul visible on board, and with their riding lights paling their ineffectual fires before the coming dawn, making up a picture refreshing to think of here in the turmoil and bustle of busy London.

All these poetical reflections were suddenly cut short by the discovery that the ship's dog was missing, but we soon found him still fast to his rope's end, and doing his level best to swim as he was towing astern. A good, plucky little "dawg" he was, and often used to look puzzled at the queer goings on of the crew of the *Teal*.

These early morning trips into moorings are so pleasant that they quite atone for the extra trouble of having to wait for water into Leigh, and the journey up to town, which is a nuisance in the evening when one is tired, becomes a pleasure in the morning by the early train, which lands one at Fenchurch Street a little before nine, in time for a good start at the week's work.

We shall now devote a few lines to the Ray, or Hadleigh Ray, which is a channel running parallel to the Thames, but separated from it at low water by a long sand which runs off from the point of Canvey Island (where it, the sand, is three-quarters of a mile wide), down to Southend Pier, where it ends, and the Ray joins the river. The pier crosses its mouth, leaving an entrance round the Leigh spit buoy. Hadleigh Ray runs in a westerly direction inside Canvey Island to Benfleet, and then bends to the southward and opens into Hole Haven. There is water in the Ray right up to the point of the Island called by the Leigh people the marsh end (mush-eend is the native pronunciation), and small craft can anchor inside of the extreme point in four feet of water, and lie sheltered from all but easterly winds. Above this point it goes adry at low water, but the island can be circumnavigated at spring tides.

The Ray is a very useful anchorage for the night for a vessel belated on the way up the river, and it offers an alternative to pushing on to Hole Haven; and it is also a very useful starting point for a long expedition down Swin to Burnham, or Brightlingsea, or Harwich. It is always very much quieter inside than it is off Southend Pier, and one can have a sound sleep in peace, instead of that dog-like dozing which is its substitute when one lies in an exposed berth on any but the very calmest of nights.

Strangers appear to regard the Ray with suspicion, if one may judge from the fact that they usually bring up outside off the pier end, where they roll and pitch in the lop, when by running round the Leigh spit buoy they could have smooth water. There is no difficulty about entering: stand boldly along the pier, well past the buoy, until the beacons on the mud are close at hand, then steer towards Leigh church. There is a thickening of the pier piles just at the turning point: keep fairly close to the beacons, which are on the north edge, and look out for two small black buoys (sewer buoys), which are also on the north edge of the water. If you are tacking, keep the pole going, and do not stand too far to the south; the sides of the channel are steep at low water, and the chief difficulty is when the flats are just covered. Half way up towards Canvey Island there is an elbow caused by a flat on the south side, and the best guide at this point is to keep among the bawleys which are afloat, avoiding any which may be aground. Near here, abreast of Crow Stone, is the entrance to Leigh Creek, with a beacon to mark it; but as there are sundry other beacons to mark mussels, etc., it is not wise for a stranger to try to get up it, for it is narrow and winding, and the tide runs swiftly up, and will put you ashore before you know where you are. Any of the bawley men who are to be found going up to Leigh with the young flood are very ready to pilot a stranger up

Hadleigh Ray

the creek for a shilling or two. Although we have known Leigh for four years, yet we still have considerable difficulty in worming the *Teal* up Leigh Creek, and on the rare occasions when we have been able to pull it off all right, we feel pleased with ourselves for the rest of the day.

Of late the entrance to the Ray and the whole lower part of it, from Southend Pier to Leigh Creek entrance (Leigh Swatch), have been silting up, and a new channel, called the Low Way, is forming. It seems probable that this Low Way will soon be the main entrance to the Ray—even now an immense body of water runs out through it; and it is gradually working down towards Southend Pier through erosion of its eastern bank and filling up of its western, a process which can be seen at low-water time to be in active progress; the west side is flat and sandy, while the east is steep, like a cutting, revealing strata of mud and sand, with ancient beds of shells laid bare by the scour of the tide.

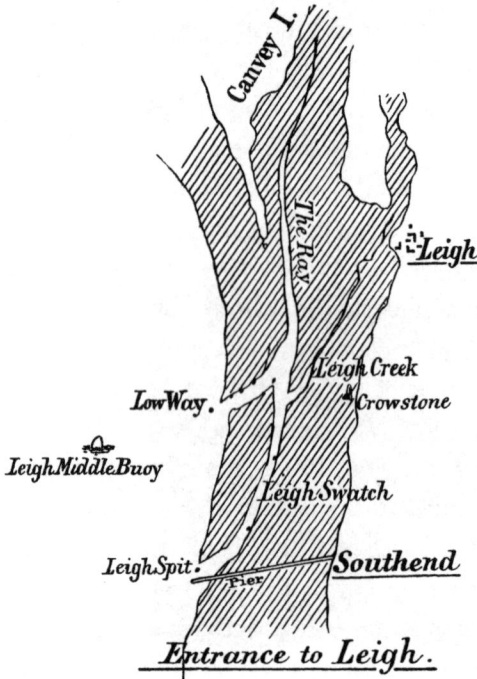

Entrance to Leigh.

The Low Way is buoyed by the harbour-master of Leigh, an ancient fisherman, who turns up once a year to levy a toll from the crew of the *Teal* for beacons to mark the creek; but the buoys (which are all on the west side, except the inmost of all) are small and hard to see until they are close aboard. Roughly, the guide to the Low Way is as follows: Take a line from Leigh middle buoy to a brickfield west of Crow Stone, and you will find the outer buoy. Then steer for Leigh Church, following the line of the buoys, and keeping them on the port hand until the Ray Channel opens with the bawleys in it. The inmost buoy is on a spit to the east of the water (see Diagram). There is a bar at the entrance to the Low Way, and the water is very shoal near the buoys, so do not go too near them.

Many a pleasant summer night have we spent at anchor in Leigh Ray, listening to the distant sounds coming over the still water from the shore, or from other vessels, the clank of a windlass, the voices of bargees shouting to one another as they drift along with the tide, the noise of an oar thrown down on deck; then perhaps there comes a little draught of a land breeze making a ripple at the bows for a few minutes, and then slowly dying away into stillness again; or it freshens and the ropes flap in the nightwind against the mast pat-a-pat, pat-a-pat, which sailors call the sound of children's footsteps, and when the tide turns the slack anchor chain drags along the bottom as she slowly swings with the young flood—crr, crr, it goes. How that same sound used to worry us before we knew what it meant, for it always filled us with the liveliest apprehensions of dragging our anchor. Both of us would awake from the soundest sleep directly it began. "Hang it, I say, I believe she's dragging." The partner perhaps continues to snore, or pretends to do so. The other, loath to turn out of his bed, waits a little while longer, but crrr it goes again. "Ugh! I can't stand that; must scramble out and see." No sign of dragging, a fine night, but the noise goes on at intervals; the stars blink at us, and a lark is singing somewhere high up; perhaps he can see the dawn from his elevated look-out, or perhaps he, too, has awaked from dreams of dragging anchor, and has turned out to look. Anyhow, he has a coat of down and feathers; I wish I had. The boat's all right. What nonsense! never knew that anchor drag in my life—better go below again and turn in.

Leigh is a far better place than Southend to keep a boat, because there are less loafers and less traffic, and better coastguard supervision, and the station is much nearer the water; and now that many of the fast trains stop there to take tickets, Leigh is much more accessible than it used to be.

CHAPTER III

Hole Haven ~ The Jenkin Swatchway
The North Yantlet

HOLE HAVEN IS WELL KNOWN to most frequenters of the London river, especially to those whose headquarters are higher up, and there is generally a pretty show of small craft lying there on Saturday and Sunday evenings in the summer; indeed some yachtsmen seldom get any further down the river, and some do not get so far, for they stick upon the spit at the entrance, which runs down so as to form a regular trap for boats coming from up river. There are usually some picturesque Dutch eel boats lying moored inside; they find it a convenient harbour, because the eels which they bring over from Holland will not live long in the Thames water as it is found off Billingsgate, so they keep them here in reserve, and take them up to London when wanted. These Dutch boats moor in a tier off the Custom House, and form quite a feature in the view of the river from London Bridge, with their bluff bows, bright varnished sides and long pennants. Those who penetrate further into the Haven find themselves among hulks in which are stored gunpowder, gun-cotton and blasting gelatine in immense quantities. The solitary ship-keepers on these crafts are usually delighted to have a yarn, and will even invite you on board if they are satisfied that you are not "Magenta" (query Colonel Majendie), or some other inspector in disguise; and when on board they will regale you with thrilling accounts of the quantity of explosives which they have got stowed on board under your feet, or behind the stove, or beside the paraffin lamp, or, at any rate, in what seems to the unaccustomed visitor to be an unpleasant proximity to himself, until he begins to wish himself safe out of Hole Haven, and feels by anticipation a sensation of being propelled through space like a sky-rocket.

At low water Hole Haven is like a huge gutter with steep sides, and there is some risk lest a stranger should anchor on the edge of the shelf, and find himself at low water sliding down a slope of fifty degrees in a very awkward fix (there is less fear of this in that part of the Haven between the entrance and the first powder hulk than there is further up). We once escaped this accident more by good luck than anything else. It was at Easter time, cold, with a strong east wind, and when we got to Leigh and made a start, the sight of steamers brought up in Sea Reach waiting for it to moderate, together with a sample of the weather off Southend Pier, made us feel diffident about putting our noses outside into the channel. The tides were very good, so we determined to attempt the perils of the north-west passage round Canvey Island, and bearing up we came along past Benfleet in fine style, only sticking fast once, and that was near the entrance into Hole Haven; we got off again though, as soon as we had learnt from a rustic on the bank that the deep water lay on his side of us. In the afternoon, when the tide had ebbed, we walked round to view the scene of the grounding, and discovered our keel marks upon a salting, and the channel close by narrow and deep, like the gorge of a mountain torrent. After getting clear we soon came out into Hole Haven, which, as it was high water, looked like an inland sea, and keeping her close to the wind, we stood along the weather shore until we were opposite a powder hulk, when we resolved to bring up, but having espied a post sticking up from the water close to us, we sounded in four or five feet, and therefore let her blow off a little before letting go the anchor; soon we had no bottom with the sounding pole, so down went the anchor, amid frantic gesticulations and shouting from a neighbouring gunpowder ship captain. We could not make out a word he said, by reason of the strong wind, but he was trying to warn us not to anchor too soon; fortunately we were clear of the shelf, which must be at least twenty feet high at that place. How annoying it is to be shouted at by unintelligible people at critical moments. One feels that one is doing something wrong, may be suicidal; one feels that they know all about it, and are proffering the most excellent advice, and yet, after all, one has to act for one's self and chance the consequences. When the tide had ebbed, we put on sea-boots and went for a visit to the powder hulk, and received a cordial invitation to come on board, which we did later on, and then we went and had a look at the river, and wondered what kind of weather we should have next day. It did not look very promising to see a great training brigantine labouring and pitching as she tacked down past the entrance to the Haven under a lower topsail, inner jib, and spanker, and we congratulated ourselves on being snug in harbour, and dolefully thought of the morrow, when we feared that we should be catching a similar or worse dusting on the way down to Sheerness.

Our worthy explosionist entertained us in the evening with the usual conversation, shouting out all his remarks at the top of his voice, even when we were sitting together in his tiny cabin. We thought he did this by way of practice, in order that when at length his cargo blew up, he might make his last words heard amid the crash of worlds. It is pleasant to take a walk on shore, and have a look at the island and the inn, with its quaint, low-ceiled rooms, which stand well below high-water mark. Here the rigours of sea cookery can be conveniently mitigated by a dinner on shore, for Mrs. Beckwith's table is excellent, even if it be a trifle primitive. This inn seems to do a large trade for such a remote place; the front door opens into a low room with benches around it, on which sits rows of bargees engaged in a never-ending debate, each with a quart mug of beer in his hand, for they despise any smaller vessel. In the parlour is a very fine specimen of a visitors' book, full of graphic tales of yacht cruises, and eke with illustrations. One would think from the logs therein written that the weather in these parts must be extremely stormy, for nearly every visitor has a tale, the good old tale, to tell of close reefs, heavy seas, cracking on and thrashing through, till one sincerely hopes that the mothers and fathers of the young and gallant yachtsmen may never see this visitors' book, and learn how great are the perils of the stormy Thames.

Hole Haven is, I think, at its best in the evening, when all is calm and peaceful, and the tuneful Dutchman can be heard serenading the stars upon his concertina, smoking the mellow Canaster all the while. When ancient mythology comes to be rewritten, and brought up to date, and the number of the Muses increased to suit modern developments, then shall the Muse of Sea-song be drawn and represented with a concertina. Was there ever a vessel without a concertina in the forecastle? We feel sure that Orpheus must have had one when he went on that buccaneering expedition with the Argonauts,

Hole Haven, Evening

to say nothing of Arion and his music on the back of the dolphin. Even here, in smoky London, the concertina which goes along the street at midnight past my chambers calls up soft memories of one of Green's good Australian clippers, and of balmy nights in the south-east trade wind, as she slipped along with all sail set, and the shreds of some ancient polka tuning up the while in the soft air of the first watch, and the Southern Cross . . . but there, my partner, who is nothing if not practical, is beginning to scoff, and wants to know who she was, and if I squeezed her hand!

A short distance from Hole Haven, on the island, there is a curious little round building, which is believed to have been built by the Dutch, who embanked and reclaimed Canvey Island, under the direction of Cornelius Vermuyden, in the time of King James the First.

In entering Hole Haven keep close to the east side, and if it is full of craft you can stand on a little way past the eel boats, and yet lie afloat at low water; this is a very good plan, unless one proposes to spend the evening ashore in the public-house, and wishes to be anchored near the landing-stage.

In going up to Hole Haven from below during the ebb, hug the opposite or south shore until reaching the Middle or even the East Blyth buoy, and then cut across, for the ebb runs very strongly to the last on the Canvey island side right down to the Chapman: a bit of a lesson which we learnt at the cost of three hours or so one Saturday night, when it was fine and calm, and we had crossed over from the other side too soon, and found the wind falling lighter and lighter, and ourselves drifting down and down to the Chapman. By the time we reached the north side we had been set down quite to the lighthouse, and the wind was all gone, and it was a case of out oars and row; it seemed as if the last drain of the ebb would never be done. Glad we were at last to find our bowsprit heading into the Haven, and to hear the rattle of the chain as we anchored in a snug berth, a hundred yards beyond Mr. Beckwith's Inn. About midway along Canvey Island, between Hole Haven and the Chapman, there is a queer beacon on shore, looking just like a milliner's lay figure; what its exact meaning is we have not been able to discover, although we tried to find out from a Coastguard officer at Hole Haven; he said it was a landmark for the purposes of navigation, but when pressed to say what its exact use was, he told us we would find it in the charts, and finally admitted, on further cross-examination, that he did not know what it was for.

To reach Hole Haven by land it is necessary to stop at Benfleet Station, and cross the ford or ferry on to Canvey Island. Benfleet is a very pretty little village, and the view from the railway where it crosses the creek is well known from one of Mr. Wyllie's drawings. Benfleet, formerly called Bemflete, was once an important place, and its name means that there was a large trade in timber (beams) there.

At Benfleet one begins to feel the sweet influence of the Thames estuary, and to sniff the ozone, or the mud, or whatever it may be; for it is the station next before Leigh, and it has a salt-water creek (Tewk's Creek), and barges come into view, soon to be succeeded by the first glimpse of the fleet of bawleys, which lie at anchor in the Ray opposite Leigh.

The distance from Hole Haven to the Medway is nine miles through the Jenkin Swatchway, and it is a good plan to take the last of the ebb down and the first of the flood up the other river, or, at least, to arrange one's time of starting in such a way as to get the help of the tide where the wind is foul, that is to say, to go down the Thames on the ebb in easterly weather, or to go up the Medway with the flood in westerly. The tide sets in and out of the mouth of the river Medway with great force, and it is not easy to stem it without a fair slant of wind.

At high water a lot of distance may be saved by crossing the Grain spit close in shore; the land may be hugged in four feet, of course keeping the sounding pole or lead going. There are some stakes close to the Martello Tower, and a causeway inside between the tower and the shore, which is hard, but not much shallower than the rest, otherwise the spit is free from obstructions. It is generally safe in small craft to cross at the Grain edge buoy, for the Grain spit lies in nine feet, and has more than enough water. The best guide for crossing the sand is to watch the movements of the barges, and to keep the sounding pole going. It must not be run too fine, as the sand is a little higher on the Medway side than upon the side of the Jenkin Swatchway.

The Jenkin Swatchway is a channel which cuts across the neck of the Nore sand, which in its turn is the continuation of the spit running off from the Isle of Grain; according to the general rule that wherever two streams join there will be a spit extending down stream from the point between them,[1] and these spits may be great or small; for instance, the Nore Sand and Grain spit together run out about three miles from the point of the Isle of Grain, and the Whitaker spit, at the junction of the West Swin Channel and the Burnham river, runs off for seven miles from Foulness Point. Swatchways, for the name is very common all round the coast, are low places which form channels or short cuts across long spits of sand.

The various names which occur in charts, such as Swatchway or Swash-way, Gatway, Sledway or Slade, Yantlet, Horse, Cant, Swin, Knock, are all very interesting etymologically, and their derivation or exact meaning often-times proves a puzzler. There is one word used by sailors which is very per-plexing, and, so far as I know, nobody can explain its origin. We were sailing with a fisherman on the Medway when we were overtaken and passed by the pilot cutter, whereupon my sailorman said, "We can't do better than follow him, and steer as he does, for he knows the tides to an *Iffygraffy*" I am told that there is even a further elaboration, and that the phrase is sometimes "the eighth of an iffygraffy", which certainly sounds very precise. Another mys-terious word of Benson's is one used by him to signify a special preparation of pitch used for stopping leaks; what the word really is we never could make out—it sounds something like Beaumatique; perhaps some of our readers may be able to throw light upon it.

The Jenkin is a little patch at the upper end of the Nore Sand, and the Jenkin buoy marks the best water; the proper side of it is the west, but either side does, and the line through the Swatchway is from the buoy to Warden Point, or to the Grain spit buoy. The south side of the Channel shoals very gradually, but the Nore side is steeper, and in tacking through it some caution must be exercised. The barges which are always passing in fleets through this

---

1   "Where a place is sheltered from the current, as at the point between the Thames and Med-way, there a shelf, as at the Nore, grows."—Roger North.

Dutch House, Canvey Island

channel often get ashore on one side or the other; and when following them it is as well for the boat sailor to remember that if they are light they may be drawing less water than he does, and if they are not actually sailing it is as well to be sure they are afloat before venturing too near them, or you may learn too late, by an unpleasant bump and general arrest of motion, that they are on the ground, and that you are in a similar predicament. In following the lead of boats under way, it is a good general rule to do it with caution. Once when the faithful Benson was aboard, he was taking us across the lower end of the Nore in just our water, and there was a rather bigger vessel following us; suddenly she struck the ground with a terrific bump, which sent her crew staggering forward along her deck, and almost took the mast out of her, and the wily Benson, who had apparently been waiting for this catastrophe, chuckled in a most unholy manner, and said, "I reckon we've took them chaps in this time." His thoughts were far away back in the days of his youth, when tradition says that the Leigh men used to anchor in little creeks and swins on the Maplin, and show a riding light at night, that the collier brigs might think there was deep water where they saw the lights. In this way profitable salvage operations were brought about sometimes.

Between Hole Haven and Sheerness there is a little creek on the south side of the Thames called the North Yantlet; it runs in close to the Yantlet buoy, and it is worth exploring, for it might prove a convenient harbour at times for a little boat in bad weather. It is marked by two beacons—one is a stone pillar, like the Crowstone on the opposite shore of the Thames, to mark the former limit of jurisdiction of the Lord Mayor and of the Thames Conservancy, while the other is an iron beacon. This creek formerly communicated with the South Yantlet, which opens into the Medway. It is not now possible to get through the Yantlets by boat, as the channel is crossed by the road and the railway, and has been filled up at these points, and it seems to be silting up generally now that there is no through current. There are plenty of wild fowl all along the North Yantlet—herons, ducks, curlew, oxbirds, and so on, and it should be a fine place for gunning. We have often used the North Yantlet as a harbour for the night, and on one trip we had a rare struggle to

get in on the ebb tide. We had started away from Hole Haven early one afternoon at high water, with a light north-west air, hoping to reach the Medway,
or perhaps the East Swale, but before we were more than half way down to the
Chapman the wind all vanished, it fell calm, and then came up very thick and
rainy. We were in the middle of the river, and when we found that the glim-
mering landscape was rapidly fading from our sight, we judged it was wise
to steer to the southward, in order to get out of the steamer lane, and also to
avoid being carried down by the ebb below the Jenkin on to the wrong side of
the Nore sand. After sundry spells of drifting and struggling with the oars in
the rain, and trying to persuade ourselves that we were enjoying it, the Yantlet
buoy loomed up suddenly close ahead of us, with the ebb sweeping past it at
a great rate, and we decided that we would have a try to get in to the North
Yantlet creek, because the afternoon was fast passing away, as it usually does
when one is becalmed, and because the only other plan was not very attractive, namely, to drift down to the mouth of the Medway, anchor there until
low water, and then to drift into the Medway after dark when the flood began to make up. As we had been late under way the previous evening, during
that row against the ebb into the Hole Haven, we both felt degenerate, and
rather hankered for a quiet evening; and there was every promise of the calm
continuing, and so with frantic efforts we rowed the *Teal* well in towards the
shore without being swept quite past the creek, and then a light breath of air
from west-south-west gave her a help in close-hauled. It was an exciting moment; should we fetch in at all? Was there water for us if we could fetch in?
Should we get on the mud, and remain aground on our bilge for six or seven
hours? However, we decided to put her at it, and were showing signs of getting in all right when the boathook fell overboard, just off the mouth of the
creek; we were using it to sound with, and it slipped. This disaster threatened
to spoil the whole affair, but we tacked about, picked up the boathook without
losing very much ground, and finally with the light draught of air we slowly
stemmed the current out of the creek, keeping near the weather shore, and
poling and rowing when the wind failed. The tide had ebbed for nearly three
hours, so there was not much water to spare, but by good luck we managed

to scrape in and reach our anchorage, just in the bend above the coastguard ship. After the usual visit from these gentry, we cooked our supper, and then, finding the rain was over, we took an exploratory journey in the Berthon to the mouth of the creek, as it was nearly low water, and we wanted to study its anatomy. We found that there was a foot of water in the channel at its mouth, and that it bent away to the eastward outside the beacons, running for a quarter of a mile nearly parallel to the shore, and finally turning north again to join the river, about halfway between the Yantlet and the Jenkin buoys; the reason of this bend being that there is a sand bank right opposite the creek's mouth. Having explored so far, we got back to our ship, for the passenger was a bit fearful of being compelled to walk back, as he had no sea-boots, and had found out from the inspection of a specimen of the bottom on the end of an oar that the mud was soft and black. He was a learned and scientific passenger, for he proved by Cosine x that the boat would not ebb dry, and he calculated the time of exposure for his photographic plates by logarithms and a slide rule which he keeps in a special pocket, as it is a foot long. Truly a mathematician is very useful on a small boat, especially if he be active and muscular. Well, we rowed back all right, and then began manoeuvres of a mysterious kind. We were in a given creek a which had a transverse measurement of x—no, not all that. We had to do something to ensure our swinging clear of the anchor, and also clear of the bank when the tide turned and began to make into the creek again; so having previously hove short while she was afloat, we got the anchor up now that she was aground, and let it go again just over her counter on the port side as she lay head up stream, and then we went below, battened her down, lighted the photographic red lamp and changed plates, accomplishing the task just before reaching the stage of asphyxia, then turned into bed, having calculated by logarithms the exact moment at which we must awake to catch the last of the water out in the morning. She swung all right in the night, and we got out without adventure, sailing until the hand-lead told us we were over the sandbank outside; then we anchored and cooked breakfast, and made elaborate preparations for a lazy and delicious day. It was calm, hazy and very hot, and after breakfast we had a swim and a run upon the Yantlet sandbank as soon as it was dry, and continued the exploration of the creek's entrance, which we had begun the evening before.

In Yantlet Creek the place to anchor is just a hundred yards beyond the Coastguard house, where there is a slight bend in the channel; the deepest water is near the west side, and there a boat drawing three feet will just touch at low water, but will not take any list. The first of the flood runs very strongly, and sets towards the west side round the bend. If the boat have too much chain out, she may swing her counter against the shore and jam across the stream. This happened to us one night, and, as usual, we both awoke at the same moment and scrambled on deck. Seeing what was wrong, almost without a word spoken, one of us ran forward to the cable, and slacked off a few feet handsomely, while the other shoved her stern off from the stone heap against which it had jammed; and with a swirl and a gurgle she swung round head to tide, and we both bundled below again out of the cold in double quick time, and in five minutes were fast asleep once more.

CHAPTER IV

The River Medway ~ Sheerness ~ Port Victoria
Stangate Creek ~ Colemouth ~ Long Reach
Cockham Wood ~ Chatham ~ The Upper Medway

WHEN ONE'S LITTLE VESSEL HAS SAFELY CROSSED the dangers of the Grain Spit, and is running into the Medway with a fair wind, there is time to take a look round, and feast one's eyes upon the moving panorama of shipping.

On the east side there is the fort on Garrison Point, and the dockyards, and the big iron sheers towering high above all the buildings; on the west side there is the old Martello tower, with Cockleshell Hard and Port Victoria beyond. In the middle, the guardship *Duncan*, a screw frigate of the early days of steam, used to swing to the tide at her moorings until quite lately. Round about there lie other men-of-war, some large and some small; a liner, or swift cruiser, or a torpedo catcher, and a training schooner flying the pennant; then there is the Chatham steamer alongside the pier taking in or discharging passengers, and a fleet of barges coming out or running into the river in procession from the Medway to the Thames, or from the Thames to the Medway; a Norwegian timber-laden brig or schooner, and a ketch or two from some of the ports on the east coast, are usually to be seen brought up off Cockleshell Hard.

To the southward can be descried the beacon which marks the entrance to the Queenborough Swale, where the Flushing steamers lie, and in the distance beyond are the hills of Kent.

The Medway in its lower reaches is a splendid cruising ground for small craft, certainly there is no other place at once so accessible from London and so convenient for small-boat sailing. From Rochester Bridge to Sheerness there are nearly fourteen miles of water, all open except in the neighbourhood of Rochester itself, where the hills and houses make the wind come rather puffy. For the rest of the distance the banks are low, so that the winds blow true and without squalls; there is soft bottom everywhere, so that no harm can follow from any accidental going ashore, and for a large part of the distance, in fact for nearly the whole way from Gillingham to Sheerness, there are a series of side creeks and channels, along which the man who is fond of exploring expeditions can penetrate into no end of quaint corners, and can find plenty of quiet anchorages for the night without alarms of any sort. The view of this part of the Medway from Brompton Lines, or from the top of Chatham Hill, shows a vast expanse of water, more like an elongated lake dotted with islands than the course of a river; and the absence of steamboat traffic lends a further charm to the Medway for the amateur boat sailor. Practically there is none; an average of about one coasting steamer per diem representing the business of the port, and this is a very different state of affairs from that which is found upon the Thames, where the steamboats, large and small, form a continuous procession up and down the river, keeping the yachtsman in a state of constant apprehension, as they bear down towards him yawing from side to side till he hardly knows whether to stand on or tack about. Then the tides do not run so hard in the Medway, and there is a capital train service between London and Chatham.

Sheerness, at the entrance to the river, does not afford much of a harbour to little craft, for it is exposed to westerly winds, and indeed we have heard of bawleys foundering there at their anchors in bad weather; but when it is fine and during the easterly winds which prevail in the spring and early summer, it is often a convenient place to bring up at. There is room close to the northward of the jetty for a few craft, but much more room on its south and better side, along the edge of the Lapwell—a mud bank which extends from Sheerness to Queenborough, and dries out at low water nearly to the end of the pier. By anchoring close inside of the head of the pier one can be out of the way, and handy, if one wants a waterman for a put ashore, or to look after the boat while the crew goes up into the town.

Most necessary stores can be bought at Sheerness, and there is a very fair hotel, the Fountain, close to the pier, if the Corinthian wants a change of diet after a few days of victual of his own cooking, or hankers after a freshwater bath to wash away what Dana calls the "sea black." It is a commonly accepted belief that in small boats everything is kept bright and clean, save and except the crew, but this is a libel; all the same a fresh-water bath is doubly delightful after a few days of salt-water washing, and it is quite the correct thing to do, for we are told that Ulysses always went in for a fresh-water bath first thing, and warm too, whenever he put into a friendly port during his long cruise home from Troy.

In the summer time Sheerness is full of London holiday makers, but they chiefly congregate about a mile further on, outside the fortifications and the moat. Here the shops are rather better, and there is more variety in the way of fruit-shops and pastry-cooks, if the ship's stores need a new supply. This part of the town has a slightly better claim to the title of Sheerness-on-Sea, and boasts of a beach fronting the Thames. At low tide there is more beach than sea, and it is very flat, and cannot be approached from the sea without great caution, except at high water; there are also posts which stick up here and there, to the terror of the navigator; to say nothing of volunteers, who fire shot and shell all over the place on Bank Holidays. Opposite Sheerness Pier is Cockleshell Hard, and close by it is Port Victoria, at the point where the river bends to the north-east on its way to the sea, and this is used to a certain extent as an anchorage by yachts; two or three may be seen there on Saturday and Sunday in the summer. For little craft it is a roadstead rather than a harbour.

Cockleshell Hard is a very nice quiet spot to anchor in to wait for the tide; it is fairly steep-to, and there is a pleasant patch of shelly beach to walk upon. A few barges and schooners may always be seen at anchor near there; we have never stayed in this berth all night, from an idea that vessels coming in at night to bring up might run into us in the dark, but we often stop to land there. At Port Victoria the South Eastern Railway have a forlorn sort of terminus, and there is a weatherboard hotel, suggesting the backwoods, where one can get food and drinks and stores. There is also a steamboat to ferry passengers across to Sheerness.

It is reported that jetties are to be built here for coaling purposes; if this is so, the place will become altered from its present peaceful and slumbering condition. We suppose that jetties will take the place of the two or three picturesque old hulks which now lie moored off here in Saltpan Reach. One of them, the *Dido*, is said to have been once a ship of Nelson's.

The railway officials at Port Victoria seem to be keen sportsmen, for we have seen them all thrown into a wild state of excitement by the sight of a flock of geese flying over the river. One bitterly cold day in January, we were standing at the station waiting for a train, and talking to the station-master, when some birds appeared flying along in the distance; he saw them, and dived into his office for a field-glass, and after a prolonged gaze at them said, "They are geese, sir." In a moment, train and steamer both forgotten, all hands and the cook were busy watching the birds, speculating, most probably, upon the chances of getting a shot at them that night after dark.

From Port Victoria, on the north side, the bank of Saltpan Reach is steep until Colemouth Creek is reached; on the south side there is the entrance to Queenborough, marked by a beacon on a spit which goes adry, and further on there is Stangate Creek entrance, marked by a buoy at the end of the spit which lies on its west side.

Stangate Creek is nearly opposite Port Victoria, and runs in a southerly direction from the Medway for over a mile; it then divides into three arms, the central one going on to Lower Halstow, the other two winding and branching until they are lost in the marshes. There is deep water (three or four fathoms) right down to the point where the creek divides; beyond that the water shoals, and before Lower Halstow is reached the channel ebbs dry at low water. Long ago, Stangate Creek was full of hulks, and was used as a quarantine station, and at the time of the Crimean war there was a large number of Russian prisoners kept there. When any of them died they were buried on the island, between Stangate and Queenborough, which has the name of Dead Man's Island. Tradition says that the fishermen used to dig up the coffins for the sake of the oak planks of which they were made; and Benson says he once picked up on the shore there a hollow thing which he used for a bailer for some time, until he discovered that it was a piece of human skull, and hastily threw it overboard.

There is an old gentleman in Rochester who has many, though vague, recollections of Stangate Creek; when a lad he lived there, on board one of the
hulks, where his father was medical officer, and he and the other lads seem
to have had fine times, with boating expeditions to Sheerness or to Chatham,
to relieve the monotony of their existence. Long after these hulks had been
removed their moorings were still there, but they have been taken up, and
there is now nothing to be seen in the creek except one buoy just inside the
entrance, and a few floating spar buoys, a little further on, to mark the limits
of the oyster grounds, which occupy much of the shores of this creek and of
its branches. The great charm of the creek is its peace and quiet, with nothing
on the move, except when now and then a great barge goes stealing along to
Halstow, or when one of the dilapidated old boats from Twinney Creek makes
a start with trawl or dredger; but these only emphasize the general calm of
things; generally one can slip in through the entrance, and have this lovely
expanse of water all to oneself, and I have spent entire days there.

One of our first serious expeditions from Chatham was into this creek,
which looked so fine on the chart, and appeared so entirely a "mare incog-
nitum" to the yachtsmen of the Medway. There were many who said they
knew it, and that it was a fine place, but none had any details to furnish; accordingly, one hot day in August, the *Wild Rose* was victualled for a two days'
cruise, a blanket was put on board, and she left Chatham at high water, with
a passenger bound for Queenborough. There was a light easterly breeze. The
dockyard sheds were quivering in the haze, and the barges were just drifting
slowly along in the tide off Upnor, as we crept down; at length we anchored at
Queenborough about five p.m.; the passenger went ashore to catch his train,
and I felt for the first time the pleasure of being out alone in my own craft,
and set to work to cook supper, then smoked a pipe, and turned in to sleep
on board. The sleeping accommodation was limited, but what of that? There
were jibs to lie upon inside the cuddy "forrard," and a blanket to wrap oneself
up in; and although it was necessary to creep into the cuddy feet first, and
to lie like a hermit crab, with one's head just inside the cuddy door, yet the
novelty of the situation was a joy that left no room for thoughts of discomfort,

even though the luff rope of that jib would persist in finding out all the tender points of the small of one's back; and so to sleep, the kind of sleep which belongs to single-handed cruising, with a sort of dog's watchfulness for the approach of other vessels, for the swinging of the boat when the tide turned, and generally for any sound of alarm by night. However, next morning the *Wild Rose* was still in the same place, and had not dragged her anchor; the day was fine and calm, and the crew ready for a swim, and then an hour of ebb was left for getting out of the Swale into the Medway. She drifted out, and slowly began her way towards Stangate Creek, and the day grew hotter and hotter, until at last another swim was resolved on, and the subsequent dressing went no further than the putting on of shirt and hat, in which appropriate garb we slowly slipped into the creek. Nothing was moving, except a few people on shore digging mud for a barge, and along the edge of the water were herons, standing still like fakirs at their prayers, and the young wild ducks swimming about would hardly deign to get out of the way of the boat, as I stood quite quiet at the tiller and steered for them. So entirely jolly was it that it was not till three o'clock in the afternoon that I began to realise how the time was going, and that the chances of getting up to Chatham that night against the ebb were pretty slender. As the wind was north-east and very light, it was time, to wake up and face the realities of the situation, so setting up the halyards, and trimming sail carefully, the *Wild Rose* at last crept out of the creek, and turned her head for home; by-and-bye the easterly air died away, and a south-west wind sprang up instead; though it was foul, yet she slipped along faster, and by a diligent working of the slack water we got up to the forts below Gillingham, and there met the *Teal*, running merrily down on the ebb to Colemouth Creek. Turning a deaf ear to the syren voices on board of her, we stood for home, but when under Cockham Wood the wind failed altogether, and there was nothing for it but to come to anchor, and postpone the return till the next day. By this time I had had enough of being all alone, and began to feel that I had heaps to say, if only there had been anyone to say it all to; and also, I began to wish that I had not forgotten the salt before leaving home. According to the boys' books, one should use gunpowder as a condiment when salt is scarce, but there was no gunpowder on board either; however, I had supper without salt, and resolved to get up early in the morning to take the last of the flood to Chatham, in order to be in time for some friends who had arranged to come down for a sail that day. I slept so soundly that I did not wake until very nearly high water, and only just managed to get to the Sun Pier against the first of the ebb, when I clambered on shore, to find everybody fast asleep, and several hours to wait before breakfast-time. In those days, it used to be the custom for two or three faithful friends from London to turn up at Chatham by the early train on certain Sunday mornings, in time for breakfast, and go for a wicked sail afterwards, and this was a day when I expected some of them down, and by 9.30 the faithful Simpson was putting us on board; he had soon discovered that the *Wild Rose* had arrived home. I remember we had on that day a first voyager of thirteen or fourteen stone, valuable, as it turned out, as well for ballast as for genial qualities of mind, for there was a strong wind all day. He had lately come back from a cruise in Norfolk Waters on board a pleasure wherry. After watching all the manoeuvres that the amateur crew were put through, of getting under way from a crowded anchorage, bringing up, and tacking and wearing ship, in silence, but with close attention, he at length grasped the meaning and value of the head sails, and was heard to murmur, "This is something like sailing. A wherry is no more good than a water-omnibus."

And here it is necessary to relieve my mind, and perhaps bore my readers, by firing off some views upon Stangate Creek as a place for the head-quarters of a yacht club. The question where to keep one's vessel is one which deeply vexes the soul of the London boat sailors, and especially of those whose boats are small, and who cannot afford the luxury of a paid hand for the season. Many a man is kept from becoming an owner by this difficulty, and there is no place up the Thames or Medway which can be considered free from objections. Leigh is bad enough, because of the short period of each tide during which there is water over the flats; the river above Gravesend has always seemed to us intolerable because of the crowds of shipping, and because of the time wasted before open and clean salt water can be reached. At Chatham there is no room, and the same may be said of Gravesend and Queenborough, and at Sheerness there is no shelter. Stangate Creek is the very place, but at present is inaccessible. What is wanted is a combination of the London yacht clubs and owners of small craft into one large and wealthy association; they could then afford to create superb head-quarters in Stangate Creek, and set free their members from the many and grievous inconveniences under which they now labour up t'other river. All that is wanted to make Stangate Creek accessible is a launch to ferry men over from Port Victoria station, and to take them aboard their own craft; an old hulk might be easily bought at small cost (they are ridiculously cheap), and fitted up as head-quarters afloat in the creek. The Medway alone offers a field for a whole year of Saturdays to Mondays, and there is the Swale available as well, for the days when the Corinthian might not care to venture out into the vasty deep outside the mouth of the river; besides, what an advantageous starting-place it is for journeys to the Essex rivers and coast. This scheme is really practicable, and would be worthy of a combination of London small craft sailor men, if only somebody with enterprise and enthusiasm would take it fairly in hand, and now is the time to do it. Soon it will be too late, as anyone can see who has noted with horror the appearance in so many creeks of an eruption of signboards threatening all manner of legal proceedings against those who may anchor there, and damage some Mr. Snook's oyster grounds. Let the London boat sailors take the matter seriously in hand, and success is assured.

There is another jolly little creek on the north side of Saltpan Reach, called Colemouth Creek, or the South Yantlet, which corresponds to the North Yantlet opposite on the Thames side. These two creeks together cut off the Isle of Grain from the Hundred of Hoo; it is not now possible to get through this way in a boat, but formerly it must have been much wider, and was used as a regular route between the two rivers. In fact, it appears that the vessels of former days, when outward bound, used to come from the Thames to the Medway through the Yantlet (or Yenlade, as old maps spell it), and then proceed by the Swale, joining the Thames again at Whitstable, a course which seems wondrous strange in the present state of these channels, and for vessels of modern size. In the time of Edward the Third a body of six hobelers was appointed to watch the Yenlade; they seem to have been a sort of horse-coastguardsmen, for they had boats and also horses—hobby-horses, from which their name was possibly derived. The hobelers remain to this day in the hufflers, whose business it is to assist barges through Rochester Bridge; they sail about Chatham and Rochester in little lug sail craft, as handy as tops, and go aboard the barges and assist in lowering away the mast and sail, and in getting it hoisted up again when the bridges have been threaded. Many of them have a device upon their sail for the bargee-skippers to know them by. One of the finest events in the Rochester Regatta is the Hufflers' Race, for they are past masters in the art of handling small boats. There is also the verb to hovel and the noun hoveller, words signifying people who render assistance to vessels in distress, with a sort of second meaning of extorting salvage money at the same time; and the Deal boatmen who act as unlicensed pilots in the English channel are called hoblers by seamen.

Colemouth Creek may be discovered from afar off by the Watch vessel which is perched high and dry beside it, for the modern analogues of the hobelers of King Edward. There is a sand spit across the mouth on its west side; the entrance, therefore, is on the east, fairly close in, much like the entrance to Hole Haven on a small scale. There is sometimes a small beacon on the end of the spit, but sometimes, on the other hand, there is not. Once inside this, the water widens out into a little sort of lake for a hundred yards or so, and then bends to the left and becomes narrow. The anchorage is anywhere in this first portion, which usually is occupied but not filled by the Coastguard boat, lying in the middle in solitary state.

Once in here, one may sleep peacefully, however rough it may be outside, with no disturbing thought, save that one must not expect to tack out against the first of the flood unless there be a fair slant of wind; luckily, the wind does not often blow right into the entrance, which runs south-east, with a curve. An enormous board has lately been set up on the shore of this creek, warning mariners against damaging the oysters laid inside, and threatening penalties, but I believe I am correct in saying that the shellfish in question re-

A Huffler's Boat

pose round the first bend, and may accordingly be disregarded by those who go no further than the Coastguard ship. The excellent Coastguardsmen here are very friendly, and can replenish the ship's larder with bread, or fresh eggs, or fresh water.

Having ventured one evening to indulge in some light chaff at their expense, because they had got their boat stuck on the spit at the mouth of the creek, we were ourselves landed in the same quandary next morning, and the tables were effectually turned. However, we all suddenly then and there discovered that we were rather glad than sorry, and, accordingly, we started off over the marshes to Port Victoria, to enjoy the pleasures of the land on shore at Sheerness (it was Easter Monday!), returning to our retired anchorage in the evening, by which time the *Teal* was once more afloat.

In the bight where Saltpan Reach joins Kithole Reach, there is another creek which we have not yet explored, because there are wide flats all round it, and these being unknown are terrible; but the masts of barges in search of mud are usually to be seen inside, and it appears to run some distance inland.

The point opposite, Sharpness Point, is fairly steep-to, and one may hug its shore, but when round it into Kithole, the flats begin again, and the stranger must keep the hand-lead or sounding-pole going. There was a steam launch ran ashore on these flats right merrily one day as we were passing. Occasionally a fine specimen of a hollow sea will be met in Kithole. Once, in a heavy rain squall from the northward, we almost lost our way there, for it came on so thick that no shores at all could be seen, and the water came tumbling on board over both bows of the little *Wild Rose* in a manner most alarming to behold.

From Kithole there is a large creek, Half Acre Creek, running away southward to Rainham, near by which place is Upchurch, the happy hunting ground of those that love Roman pottery, with a wide mud flat, called Bishop's Ooze, between it and the main channel. On this and on many of the other outlying points in the Medway, it has been our fate, at one time or another, to spend a bad quarter of an hour, sometimes a good deal longer. It happened that I was taking a friend out for a sail, just to show him the river, and had forgotten all about Bishop's Ooze, until the *Wild Rose* suddenly stopped, and we saw where we were; and to make things worse, off went my cap while getting the sails down, and there was nothing to be done but to watch it slowly drift away to leeward over the ooze. An old friend it was, of the cheese-cutter pattern, and it had been the companion of a voyage from London to Melbourne and back in a comfortable, though leaky and ancient, clipper ship.

There is a strong tide out of Half Acre Creek on the ebb, very useful when it shoves one up to windward in tacking down the Medway with an easterly wind. Then is the time to keep the flats in one's mind, when she goes merrily along, doing a good board, lest suddenly a change come o'er the spirit of the dream, and one finds, in the words of the poet, that "the boat is still there, though the waters are gone," and ten to one, as soon as the boat is hard and fast aground, the weather begins to look threatening. One of my mathematical friends would say that this was an instance of the Law of spite, an universal natural law, which brings on rain when people go out with their best hat on and have forgotten their umbrella, and which makes it thaw as soon as you send your skates to be ground.

The course up the river through Long Reach is all plain sailing; there is deep water on the south side, and a line drawn from Okeham Ness to the forts clears the flats of the north shore. There are two red buoys at the upper and lower ends of the Mussel bank, and the shoal itself is said to go dry at low water springs, but we have never seen it so. To make quite safe, one may keep to the southward of them. When one is tired of the main channel of Long Reach, it is a change to go up Half Acre Creek and through Yantlet Creek, at the back of Darnett Fort; there is six foot least water at low tide, and snug lying for a belated wanderer on his way to Chatham, with the chance of a shot at some wild fowl early in the morning. It is also possible to sail behind Hoo Fort at high tides, but it is as well to have a leading wind and a flowing tide the first time the attempt is made. This creek is sometimes used as a short cut, and we have seen the Medway pilot cutter, *Tom King*, of twenty tons, going through, but to get stuck there with a falling tide is no joke, as it means eight or nine hours in what is, at low water, nothing but a muddy and forlorn ditch, with an amount of list which would be extremely inconvenient, not to say dangerous.

The Reach between the forts is called Pinup Reach, and is full of small buoys, which mark a torpedo mine field; many of these are small and not easily seen, but it is necessary to keep a good look out for them, as they are of iron, to say nothing of the risk of being blown up by accident in case the dynamite down below should be feeling rather more irritable than usual.

Off Hoo Fort there is a spit of stones, almost the only stones in the Medway, forming apparently an artificial causeway. It is marked at the end by an iron beacon, which usually shows signs of collisions with barges, being bent about in all kinds of ways. It is best to keep outside this always, although there may be six feet of water inside at high tide. The deepest water through Pinup is on the opposite or eastern side, but there is plenty everywhere for all but big ships, and there is slack water on the western side under the point, which is useful when working up against the ebb tide. The view of the Kentish shores from Pinup is very pretty, especially in spring, when the cherry orchards about Rainham and Gadshill (not that of Falstaff and of Charles Dickens) are in full bloom. On the top of the hill there is a great building, looking like a huge biscuit tin; this is the temple of the tribe of Jezreel, a mysterious sect of these parts which was founded by a baker of Chatham.

At Gillingham the river widens out into a bight, with flat, muddy shores, where various craft lie at anchor or at moorings. Here there are more torpedo buoys, and hulks for raising and lowering them, and the yachts of the Royal Engineer Yacht Club, the *Buccaneer*, and others, lie here. At low water there is a good deal of mud laid bare on the Gillingham side, but this does not greatly concern the passer by, for there are so many craft, hulks, buoys, lighters, and so on, that it is better not to venture in among them, but to keep in the middle of the stream. Gillingham would be a very convenient place in which to keep a yacht if it were more accessible, and the same applies to Upnor, higher up the river. It is interesting to know that, in the days of Good Queen Bess, Gillingham could boast of four quays and twenty-seven ships, most of them small craft, the largest being of twenty tons, and seventeen others of only one ton each. The dockyard basins have an entrance at Gillingham, and there is a huge crane near the entrance, which can lift hundred-ton guns and run away with them. The whole of the piece of ground from here to Chatham Reach, formerly St. Mary's Island, and now known as the Dockyard Extension, is still in process of reclamation from its original wildness, and gangs of convicts are to be seen there, with warders standing on platforms, armed with rifles to shoot at any who might try to escape by swimming across the river.

The reach above Gillingham leads past Cockham Wood to Upnor, and is the prettiest part of the river. Its north shore is steep and wooded, and out in the stream lies the old hulk *Leonidas*, red painted, and full of gunpowder. There is a gravel beach, and a wood full of nightingales. The sun mostly seems to shine here, and it is a good place to anchor in for the night, always remembering to have the riding light burning brightly, and to keep close in to the shore, on account of the barge traffic. A year or two since, three of us sailed up to Chatham, to assist at the opening cruise of the Medway Yacht Club, and also at the opening dinner to follow, finding our way back eventually to the Sun Pier at eleven p.m. After being carefully deposited on board the *Teal* from a shore boat, for it hardly seemed the time to trust one's fortunes in a seven-foot Berthon, we set jib and mizen, and with an ebb tide and a soft and gentle breeze, we soon dropped down to Cockham Wood, to find another yacht anchored there for company, and the nightingales tuning up their best, and we promptly voted it a far better berth than any among the slimy and not too fragrant mud banks and sewers of Chatham, and looked forward to a swim and a run ashore before breakfast in the morning. Another point of advantage is its freedom from morning callers. Once, when we were anchored near the Sun Pier, about five in the morning, an enterprising young ruffian thought the occasion a good one for coming alongside to prospect for moveables, little reckoning that as he touched the little vessel's sides there would emerge, Jack-in-the-boxlike, a half-dressed and dangerous looking figure from the fore hatch and another from aft, with a truculence of aspect heightened by a pair of gold spectacles; and that both, in well drilled chorus, and in accents bland, would demand an explanation of the unexpected visit. The double-barrelled apparition proved too much for our young friend; his jaw dropped, he hastily withdrew, murmuring by way of apology for his intrusion, "I say, d'yer stay out all night in that 'ere?"

It may be worth mentioning that in the lower part of Cockham Wood Reach there is a mud flat over against the village of Hoo. It begins to run out from the shore near a curious sort of patch of red brick wall, which is, as a matter of fact, the remains of a fort built in Queen Elizabeth's time, and once proudly mounting twenty-three guns, for the benefit of the adventurous Dutchmen, who were much too fond of expeditions up the Medway, which they enlivened by cannonading Sheerness, burning the fleet at Chatham, and other desperate behaviour. De Ruyter, for instance, came up in 1667, and burnt a fleet at Gillingham, and also went on to Upnor, where, perhaps, Upnor Castle may have stopped him, but for details the reader may consult Mr. Pepys' diary. I once made a visit to the old fort in Cockham Wood Reach, to see if it really was anything more than a ruined brick-kiln, as had been stoutly maintained by a Rochester friend of mine, and although there were no doubloons, nor pieces of eight lying about loose on the ground, yet there were other evidences of high civilisation in the shape of ancient broken bottles, of coarse glass and broad squat shape, such as the buccaneers of those days might have used to carry their *rhummi succus* in. "Rhummi succus" is the "orsepital name" for rum, at any rate among the initiated.

To proceed in the manner of the guide-book, the next place of interest is Upnor, which is a very pretty straggling village, unfortunately spoilt by the Stygian smoke and fume of a large cement factory at the bend in the river, which must be a great nuisance "when the east winds do blow;" and when the south or west wind takes its place, the unhappy village is again hardly out of range of other equally Stygian cementworks, for the whole Medway valley is full of them. The cement is made by grinding together three parts of chalk with one of Medway mud, and roasting it in a kiln, and the banks of the river are being dug away wholesale in places for the sake of the mud, leaving huge lagoons and making worse the already desperately bad condition of the saltings of the lower reaches of the river.

The Medway Valley

At Upnor there is a stone pillar like that at the entrance to the North Yant-let, and that one called Crow-stone, between Leigh and Southend, and here Chatham Reach opens out, running nearly north and south, and full of inter-esting sights. First and foremost the huge mooring buoys, almost as big as five-tonners, which must be carefully avoided, as they surge to and fro in the stream. Well do I remember coming back late one night, after my first cruise alone in the *Wild Rose*, how she came sliding home with a light air and a strong flood tide, and how I peered into the darkness, expecting every moment to go full butt into one of these monsters, but managed to escape, more by luck than cunning, and reached the anchorage by the Sun Pier in safety about eleven p.m. In those days she used to lie at anchor just on the edge of the mud above the pier, and nervous work it was for a beginner to get under way from there single-handed, under the scornful eye of all the long-shore loafers on the pier, and to scrape out clear between the boats and barges that constantly filled up all the room outside of the little craft. It is not so very long ago that this part of the river was full of old hulks moored in mid-stream, but, with the exception of two or three which lie just off the marine barracks, they are happily de-parted. There is still to be seen the hulk of the *Challenger*, laid up in ordinary since she came home from her scientific expedition of sixteen years ago or so. She was first pointed out to me by the trusty Simpson, dockyard labourer and ex-North Sea smacksman, who used to look after the *Wild Rose* in those days. He said: "That's the ship what 'as been further round the world than any other;" the bearings of which remark became gradually clear on learning that her name was the *Challenger*. Then there are the dockyards, with per-haps a man-of-war fitting out, and torpedo boats, and opposite is a strange looking hill, where the Royal Engineers play at engineering, with mines, and counterscarps, and fascines, and gabions, and a fortified house, and all man-ner of things.

But the joy and delight of the Medway is in its barges, as they sail in stately procession up and down the river; there is but little other traffic, save a few fishing bawleys, with over-grown topsails and tiny jibs; and an occasional col-lier steamer. Once there came a fine Greek steamer, and behold her name was

Ulysses, from the port of Ithaca. She had not come to carry off another Helen from Troy town, but merely to bring a cargo of wheat to her consignees; and although the modern screw steamship is a very different sort of craft to that in which the god-like son of Laertes used to meet such heavy weather in the Ionian Sea, yet, after all, in a fishing craft of to-day there is very little in the way of tackling but what was well within the reach of the ancients. Replace by good rope the wire shrouds and the chain cable, which are merely innovations of yesterday, and there you are. The Homeric ship seems, from the best authorities, to have been a lug-sail craft, with forestay, backstays and a lowering mast, and probably was very much like a modern Scotch fishing lugger.

The greatest trouble which a stranger meets with on his arrival at Chatham is to know where to bring up. Yachts flying the blue ensign have the privilege, it is said, of anchoring in the Gun Wharf water, or of making fast to a buoy there, but the million are warned off by a notice, "No vessel to moor to the buoys, nor to anchor off this wall." Still we believe that strangers, who can find room, and only wish to remain a short time, may anchor there unmolested if they will call and leave their cards at Gun Wharf House. Then the bight on the east side of the Sun Pier is all taken up by the Chatham bawleys when they are at home; so, although it may look a convenient spot when they are away fishing, they are certain to turn up ere long and crowd one out, to say nothing of the town sewer running in just there. There is a little room on the west side of the Sun Pier for a small craft, just near the edge of the mud, and, indeed, for one summer season the *Wild Rose* lay there at anchor. Since then the space at this point has been partly taken up by a new piece of wharf, and is not much of a berth for a stranger. There is room to be found near the new pier at Blue Boar Hard, or one may anchor further up, in the bight opposite Gas House Point, on the north or Strood side, but this is rather far away, if there is any shopping to be done. Taking all these things into consideration, the neighbourhood of Blue Boar Pier is perhaps the most convenient and quiet place to anchor in for the night.

The south or town side of the Medway as it runs through Chatham and Rochester consists largely of mud, littered up in the usual way with balks of timber, and with yachts and other craft in the various stages of decay, and having more or less rudimentary wharfs and jetties at intervals. There is no public wharf or quay, but the houses reach right down to high-water mark, Some day all this will be changed by the building out of frontages to an uniform line at low-water mark according to a prescribed scheme. A few of these have already been made, or are now in course of construction, but it will be a long time before vessels will be able to go alongside to discharge or to load their cargoes, and at present this has to be done by means of lighters.

Just below the Sun Pier there is a bight, which looks as if it were silting up more and more, and a good deal of the Gun Wharf frontage is filled up with mud, so that at low water there are twenty or thirty yards of mud left uncovered. Where the Gun Wharf stands was formerly a dock for the ships of His Majesty King James the First. At the Sun Pier there are two families of brothers, whose spare time is largely taken up by rivalry and strife; they let row boats for hire, and are very willing and obliging in looking after one's yacht, or in putting one ashore or aboard. Their names are Moore and Adams.

There are some very nice-looking tiny lug-sail boats on this part of the river, rigged with brown-tanned main and mizen; the latter a tiny pocket handkerchief shipped on the rudder post. They are about fourteen feet long, strongly built like barges' boats, and belong to the hufflers. There is another ancient type of boat still in use at Rochester, the Peter boat, which seems to be essentially a craft with stem and stern alike, and with a little deck and coamings at both ends. They are mostly rigged with a good big spritsail and foresail, the mast without shrouds, in order to unship easily. They are used for netting smelts, and the little decks are for coiling down the net, without letting a lot of water, fish and rubbish into the bottom of the boat. The fishermen at Leigh used these boats largely about sixty years ago, and there is still an inn at Leigh with "Peter Boat" for her sign, but they are a vanishing type. The boat in Turner's picture of the "Bligh Sand" is a regular Peter boat, and no doubt hailed from Leigh. They have a deep keel, running right fore and aft, and they keep a pretty straight course, even when rowed by an oar on one side only. The bawley boat, which has taken their place, is much bigger and more

Aylesford Bridge

powerful. Bawley is possibly a corruption of Bartlemey or Bartholomew, the companion of Peter. The Rochester bawleys have their mast rather further forward than those of Leigh, and can work under extremely little head sail; a tiny jib and a small foresail seeming to balance their mainsail and topsail quite well. The Chatham bawleys anchor in the bight near the Gun Wharf when they are at home, and the Rochester fleet bring up in a tier just beside the pier at Strood, where they can be inspected with advantage.

Very few salt-water craft, except the barges, venture above the bridges at Rochester; the barges, however, penetrate ever so far, even beyond Maidstone. There are three bridges, all side by side, two being for railways and the third being the renowned Rochester Bridge, which, like London Bridge and Bideford Bridge, is a landed proprietor, and gives good dinners and dispenses much money in charity. It has lands in Sheppey, in several parishes in Kent, and also a town house in London. In the time of Henry I the repairs of the bridge (then a drawbridge) were parcelled out as follows: The first land pier on the east side to the Bishop of Rochester, the second to Gillingham and Chatham, the third to the Bishop, the fourth to the King, the fifth to the Archbishop, the sixth to the tenants of Hollingbourne, the seventh and eighth to the men of Hoo, while the ninth and last on the west side was assigned to the Archbishop; this was apparently a wooden bridge. Richard II built a new stone bridge, and endowed it with lands to form the Bridge Estate, and failing that source the cost of maintenance was to devolve upon certain parishes each to be responsible for so many feet and inches of the bridge.

There is a height of about twenty feet under the centre of the arches at high water, and forty at low, and anyone who decides to explore the upper reaches will find good anchorage just above the bridge on the north side, out of the way of the traffic.

The trip up to Maidstone is worth doing, and can well be managed in a small sailing boat. The chief difficulty is found in the narrowness and emptiness of the river at low-water time, which compels one to anchor either on the soft mud, or in the middle of the stream right in the way of everything. However, there is very little traffic up there, except at tide time; from a little way above Snodland there is a towing-path. The best method of seeing this part of the river is to take the tide up from Rochester, and when sailing is no longer possible, to tow up to the lock at Allington, and stay there for the night. The island and lock-house are very pretty; there is an inn handy; above the lock, of course, the mud-banks of the tidal part come to an end, and the boat can lie alongside the meadows in clean, fresh water. There is a bridge, a very low one, at Aylesford, two miles below Allington Lock, and here the mast must be unshipped and lowered. At low water the Medway for several miles below Aylesford, and up to Allington Lock, is a deep and dreadful ditch, though it is very pretty at high water. Above Maidstone the river is rather a *terra incognita* but those who have penetrated say it is very pretty. For the first few miles out of Maidstone it looks a delightful river, peaceful and lovely. The barges manage to sail up to Wateringbury; so little yachts should also be able to do so. We have long cherished a determination to go up from Maidstone one day, armed with luncheon-basket and camera, and see whether it does not offer attractions of a quieter kind than those of the upper Thames. Maidstone, however, has very few express trains to London, and travelling by slow train, bad enough at the best of times, is particularly virulent on Sunday evenings after a tiring day on the water.

The views of the Medway Valley from the hills round Rochester are very fine, for at this point the river cuts right through the high chalk hills, and from either side the windings of the Medway, in its course between Aylesford and Rochester, can be seen as though in a map, with brown-sailed barges dotted here and there between the meadows, and with blurred masses of steam and smoke from the cement works to provide atmospheric effects, which are unfortunately for the most part too intense.

CHAPTER V

Queenborough ~ The Swale
Faversham Creek ~ Warden Point

QUEENBOROUGH IS A VERY ANCIENT TOWN, and consists mainly of one picturesque old street, and also boasts a queer little creek, dry at low water, usually having a few craft lying in it, and an old yacht or two hauled up on to the saltings upon the farther side. It looks a convenient place for laying a yacht up for the winter, and the Harbour Master undertakes to look after them if they are left in his care; and it is accessible from London, because of the fast trains which serve the Flushing mail boats. Queenborough takes its name from Queen Philippa, who landed there when she came to marry King Edward the Third, and we suppose that King's Ferry, where now is the bridge over the Swale, is named from King Edward having crossed over at that place when he came to meet his bride.

Both here and at Sheerness, situated as they are upon alluvial mud and clay, the question of the water supply seems to have been a difficulty. The people at Sheerness say their water comes from Essex, the fact being that it comes from a deep well somewhere in the town, and possibly it may find its way into the well underneath the Thames in the deep layers of the chalk; Hasted tells us that in 1723 the well at Queenborough was in an unsatisfactory state, and was opened afresh. It was found to be two hundred feet deep, and with little water, so they bored eighty-one feet more, when the auger slipped down, and up came water which proved good, "for they put some soap into it, and it lathered finely; and they boiled old peas in it, which it did well."

The entrance into the Swale is narrow, and there is a beacon and a light on a spit on its western side; the mud dries out almost, if not quite, to this beacon at low water, and it must be approached with great caution, as the channel shoals rapidly both on this and on the opposite side, where there are catchy mud flats; a little further on the huge mass of the pier effectually blocks out all the wind when it is easterly, and is apt to be a nuisance if one is creeping in against an ebb tide. In choosing a berth at Queenborough, keep to the eastern side of the channel, for the traffic passes on the western side, and bring up just outside the line of the fishing smacks. There are three or four of these in a line, which just take the ground on the edge of the water. When the tide is high, strangers are very likely to go too far in, for there is a rather wide mud flat off the town, and the fishing smacks in question appear to be lying almost in the middle. Bear in mind also that there is a stone causeway, which can be seen leading over the mud to low-water mark; its end is marked by a little can buoy, and it would be very awkward to anchor over the concrete and settle down uncomfortably on it as the tide ebbed, to say nothing of the risks of obstructing the traffic of the town, for a good many people pass along that causeway to and from the vessels and the barges. Well can we remember our troubles one cold night, anchored off Queenborough! We had come down from Hole Haven against a strong east wind, and there was a hollow sea off the lower Blyth Buoy, which ducked us all pretty effectually, in spite of oileys and sea-boots. The Berthon had been doubled up and stowed in the cabin, two reefs tied down in the mainsail, and things generally lashed and made snug, for we guessed what was in store for us; and by-and-bye we put the passenger into the cabin along with the Berthon, and battened him down too. However, she went very well, as she always did when relieved of the task of towing the boat, and under the Nore Sand the sea was smoother, and our progress better. In due time we ran into Queenborough and brought up; but did it badly, choosing a berth just ahead of a fishing smack, and not far enough ahead to be clear of her anchor. Although we felt a misgiving that all was not right, we proceeded to put on dry clothes, and as a special treat after the cold and wet, we went ashore and dined at a little inn, and there the passenger elected to sleep—wise man! Self and partner returned to the *Teal*; the tide had just turned, the boats were on the swing, the *Teal* betraying an improper affection for that horrid smack, and persistently kept sidling up alongside of it. "I say, Captain," says partner, "here's a pretty go, you have picked up a vile berth. I believe our chain is foul of theirs." "I know," replied I dolefully. Then to make things worse, that wicked *Teal* must needs try and swing round to the other side of the fishing boat, for all the world like a couple in a square dance, setting to partners. This was too dreadful, and her owners plunged into a heated argument as to which was her proper side. One thought the anchor was here, and the other thought it was there, and one was for shoving her round the bow of the vessel to clear her, while the other obstinately vowed that such an act would be fatal, by giving her chain a round turn round the other one's cable. After the discussion had continued for more than an hour, to no purpose, in the bitter cold of a night in April, we both turned in, in an unhappy frame of mind, foreseeing trouble in the morning; but it did not turn out so very badly after all, for on weighing anchor we fished up the other one's chain, and were able to clear it without much difficulty, but we had had our lesson—never to let go anchor anywhere close ahead of another vessel, but rather, if room is scarce, to go just astern of one.

People usually anchor opposite the town, and very often there is not much room to spare, and it is not very nice to have to bring up in the middle of a lot of other craft, especially when the holding ground is at all doubtful, and they do say that the mud is so soft off Queenborough that an anchor is apt to drag through it. The bight a little further on, near a funny rounded hill, looks as if it might be a good place to anchor in for a quiet night's rest, and barges sometimes choose a berth there in preference to lying off the town.

Most Thames men know the West Swale, as far as Queenborough, and plenty of other people have been by the steamers which run from there to Flushing, some of these latter, no doubt, not knowing nor caring anything about the whereabouts of the place, except that it is reached by the Chatham and Dover Railway.

It is a capital cruise round Sheppey, but it is wise to have a flowing tide, and a fair wind too, if it can be conveniently secured. It is also advisable to prepare one's mind for very probable delays—the result of running aground. The only time I ever got round without running ashore anywhere was on my first attempt, when luck, not learning, showed the way. Having advised a friend to try the voyage, he did so, and when next he met me I was greeted as follows: "Here, you're a nice sort of a man, you are, to send me into that hole of a place; I did get round, but I believe I must have scraped off half my out-side lead on the way." However, he has been there again since, and now thinks it a fine place for shooting in. What hardships some men will endure for the sake of shooting! They will cruise about in winter, spend whole days shivering in open boats, potter about for hours on mud flats, get up before dawn, and think they are enjoying themselves. "Ugh! not me; 'taint loikely. I'm fair off it. What d'yer take me for? "

The best way of going through the Swale from Queenborough is to pick a day with a nice westerly wind, and start an hour or so before high water, so as to get through the bridge with a fair tide, and carry the ebb all the way down beyond, and have plenty of water too, for this is very necessary. There are two important horses on the way to King's Ferry Bridge: keep the first on the starboard hand, and the second on the port hand, and look out for the small beacons which mark them.

At King's Ferry there are a few hufflers, as there are at Chatham, and for the same purpose—to help the barges through the bridge; for although it is a swing bridge the people in charge object to raising it for boats and vessels with lowering masts. The barge traffic through this part of the Swale is consider-able, for most of the Sittingbourne traffic passes this way, and the creek which leads to it—Milton Creek—turns off to the southward a mile or two further on. At Sittingbourne there are immense brickworks, enough by themselves to keep fleets of barges busy, carrying bricks to London, and coal back again to Sittingbourne, and there are cement works too.

The hufflers at King's Ferry have little boats, no bigger than ordinary barges' punts, but they contrive to roof in the fore part, and so make them-selves a kind of cabin, in which they can even rise to the dignity of a stove. One of them told us that there was very good fishing to be had there for whit-ing pout, but that they would only bite at slack-water time. We can answer for it that there are plenty of crabs there at any rate, by the way they swarmed round us once when we were at anchor near the edge of the mud; they simply crowded and jostled one another in their eagerness to pick up the crumbs af-ter our supper time.

The first trip round, we started off from Queenborough one morning, with a nice south-west breeze, and reached the bridge all right; then came the question, could we shoot it all standing, or must we wait for it to be raised? Finally deciding to chance it, we put the *Wild Rose* at it, the owner feeling a "leetle" bit anxious lest the head room might prove too scanty; however, it was all right, and as there was a strong wind and plenty of water, we soon reached Harty Ferry without adventure, but without learning much except the general lie of the channel, and noting the point where Milton Creek runs off towards Sittingbourne. By-the-bye, just opposite there, the flat runs out ever so far from the north side nearly across the channel, and it is a very dangerous place for getting picked up. This we know, for only last summer we spent six hours there, watching the tide ebb away from us for three hours, and flow back again for the rest of the time; it was a broiling day in August, and there was nothing to do but to slumber and sleep. On this occasion, before we went aground, the Berthon went adrift, and there was great eagerness to know who had made the painter fast. We both promptly turned upon our passenger, who, in a trembling voice, confessed that he was the man. So he was at once condemned to go overboard and swim for it, as it had drifted with the wind into shallow water; we further salved our consciences for thus making the guest walk the plank, by speciously reasoning that both our services were needed for the handling of the vessel in such critical manoeuvring in narrow waters, and we stood as near to him as we dared, and finally picked him up again, with the boat's painter in his hand. But Nemesis was upon us, and we went aground for six hours almost at once, and, in addition, discovered that our passenger could not be induced to lay hand on rope for the remainder of the cruise; but he has since learnt how to tie two half-hitches, and knows the value of a round turn, and is, therefore, a wiser and a better man. But to return to the first cruise. The party consisted of a friend, his wife, and myself; we were to go ashore at Harty Ferry, and after that F. and his wife should cross over and walk to Faversham, returning next day. By-the-bye, there is a huge horse just before Harty Ferry is reached, but there is usually water on both sides. We

A Medway Barge

anchored close to the line of the Ferry and had some luncheon, and when the ferryman passed I hailed him, and asked leave to go ashore in his flat-bottomed punt. He said "Yes," so we weighed anchor and sailed up along-side the punt; I jumped out, and cast loose the mooring for the *Wild Rose* to pick up, but to our horror and dismay it sank directly it fell into the water. However, I went ashore, bought some eggs at the Ferry House Inn, and feeling that the character of a navigator had to be kept up, I asked for rum. This tasted so soft and mild, that I felt sure it must be old (I have learnt since that this semblance of age is wickedly produced by the simple and economical method of adding water to the spirit). I said to myself, "Ah, now, this liquor has been here for ages—perhaps smuggled, too—must be fifty years old, if it's a day. What a find! I really ought to buy up their stock. One can't get such good stuff now-a-days." So I praised the rum, and ventured the suggestion that it must be old. "Yes," replied the good lady, "it is; we have had it in the house for seven weeks or more."

When the ferryman came back, and found his punt mooring was gone, there was a marked coolness; and by way of punishment, he refused to put my friend and his wife across, saying it was too late (good enough excuse for simpletons like us), so we made sail on the *Teal*, and resolved to do it ourselves, and to penetrate the unknown of Faversham Creek; and after a good deal of trouble, as the wind and tide were both against us, we succeeded in reaching a house, which we thought was Ore. By this time it was nearly low water, and Faversham Creek at low water is a poor place—a wide ditch, with steep sides and any amount of mud, but very little water. Luckily, a man hailed us, and said it was no good trying to go any further, as there was no water, so we pushed in against the bank, and my friend and his wife went ashore, while I made myself snug on board with rugs and blankets, and slept; the boat lying in mud of a rank sort, suggesting ague and quinine bitters. In the morning the scene had changed. It was high water, and the creek was bank full, and soon a tug came puffing along with a schooner in tow, then some barges and a fishing smack or two, and lastly my crew, with smiling faces; so taking a lead from a fishing boat, we came out of that creek, and out past Whitstable, and round

Warden Point to Sheerness once more. In spite of these rather muddy experiences, we still hanker for another visit to Faversham, going up with the tide, and coming away again to the Swale with the first of the ebb, so as not to get stuck fast up there.

In olden days the people of Faversham do not seem to have been very loyal to the Crown, for they dug up the coffin of King Stephen for the sake of the lead, throwing the king's body into their creek; and probably they did the same for Queen Matilda. Also, when King James the Second was about to fly the country, they seized his vessel, as it lay in the East Swale. Hasted relates the story as follows: "The Faversham sailors observing a vessel of about 30 tons lying at Shellness to take in ballast, resolved to go and board her; accordingly, they went in the evening with three smacks and about forty men, and in the cabin of it they seized three persons of quality. From them they took 300 guineas and two gold medals, and brought them all three on shore beyond Ore."—One of the three persons of quality was the king.

At the entrance to the creek there is a longish spit, marked by two little buoys, one on the side of the Swale, and one on the side of the creek. We learnt their position by trying to find the channel in between them, but were saved from mishap by some kind deity or water-nymph.

Our Swale adventures are all rather tinctured with mud, for on another memorable occasion we tried to turn up from Whitstable to Queenborough on the first of the flood, and found it rather tedious, as we were continually in advance of the water, and had to wait for it upon most of the spits and horses; but, though tedious, it was eminently instructive. Another time we slept on the Pollard Spit, all through one pitch-dark night, and this was the how and the wherefore of it. We went down, we being self and partner, to Leigh for a cruise, and with us a trusty friend from the Midland counties, sometimes called on board by the name of Hayseeds,[1] because on his first trip he betrayed an uncertainty as to which way to put the tiller. He was an ardent yachtsman, however, and soon learnt; so we did not find it necessary, as Magellan did, to

---

1   Dana, *Two Years before the Mast*—"His boat's crew were a pretty raw set, just out of the bush, and as the sailors' phrase is—Hadn't got the hayseed out of their hair."

hang up onions and garlic in the rigging as a guide to the helmsman,[1] but contented ourselves with reminding him of Mr. Reuben Ranzo:

Oh, Reuben was no sailor;
Ranzo, boys, Ranzo.
He shipped aboard a whaler;
Ranzo, boys, Ranzo.
They took him to the gangway;
Ranzo, boys, Ranzo.
And gave him forty lashes;
Ranzo, boys, Ranzo.

On reaching Leigh, we discovered the owner of the yacht, *Curlew*, four tons register, in difficulties, as there was no one to go with him; so, after a debate, we arranged that we should cruise in company—the partner to go with him for the outward journey, and I on the homeward. We bundled aboard in a hurry, and started off for the East Swale. We turned down with the ebb tide, against a southeasterly wind, but before making the Whitstable Buoy it came on dusk, and very soon grew quite dark. We were then negociating the "Columbine," and the *Curlew* was away a mile or more to leeward; the flood was making up hard; we got inside the "Columbine" all right, but found it very dark, and soon touched bottom, with only a very vague idea as to the exact place we were in; soundings showed that it was flat all round us, and we brought up to wait for water. I was reminded of the advice I once heard given by a blue-eyed and much-travelled friend of ours to some men who were starting for a trip on the Norfolk Broads; he said, "Now mind you take an anchor

---

1   Guillemard, *Life of Magellan*—"It appears that on weighing anchor, and on the pilots giving their orders, larboard or starboard, to the helmsmen, the latter were greatly embarrassed in their minds, as not being as yet learned in such expressions, and, in consequence, got into difficulties, owing to the number of craft round them; upon which, João Homem, captain of one of the caravels, ordered the pilot that he should speak to the sailors in a language that they could understand, and that when he wished to steer starboard he should say 'garlick,' and when to larboard, 'onions'; and on either side of the helm he ordered a string of these things to be hung."

with you, for then, if you get into a fix, you can stop the boat with it, and think out the matter, and settle what had better be done." We, therefore, anchored, and thought it out, and decided, first, that we were on the flats round the Pollard Spit; second, that we wanted our supper; third, that it was too dark to go away, and we were all right where we were. No sign of the *Curlew*, though we showed a light and hailed. Our voices died away across the mere. We then remembered that we had all their fresh water, and they had all our bottled beer and ginger beer.

Next morning early we weighed anchor, and cruised around in search of them, but saw no sign, and so went home to Leigh; and soon after arriving in Leigh Ray we descried them afar off, splashing along under all sail. There was a strong breeze, and she went on right past us into Leigh. They had got safely in, missing us in the dark, and had run up as far as the Coastguard Ship, off Faversham Creek, where they brought up in smooth water, while we were rolling about on the Pollard. At a Court Martial held on our return to Leigh, the partner was consequently awarded the leather medal for good navigation, and we were ordered to be reprimanded for endangering the ship, and were thereby reprimanded accordingly. The moral is, that it is difficult to enter the Swale after dark, unless you know your way, and that on the flood there is a strong set to the southward, as the tide flows in strongly over the Columbine and through Ham Gat; by daylight it is easy enough, and Ham Gat presents no difficulties. After passing Shellness the channel bends over on the south side, and on the north side of it is a horse, marked at its eastern end by a buoy. Between this sand and the north shore is a fairly snug berth to anchor in, although at high water it is not very sheltered. It is a convenient spot if one expects to have to tack out to the eastward early next day, as it gives one another hour in bed in the morning. The buoy is not at the extreme point of the horse, for this runs a little further to the east. Once we went ashore there, when running up into the Swale with the young flood. A passenger was at the helm, and having shown him the buoy, and told him which side to go, the skipper went below to fill his pipe and have a quiet smoke, but alas! for in a few minutes the steersman called out that she was aground, and so it was. There was no wind, and we soon had the anchor led aft, outside of the rigging, and dropped it overboard under her stern, to keep her from being set further on. The skipper was wroth, but dissembled, reproaching himself for leaving the bridge while going into port; but when a man came rowing off from a brig which lay at anchor about half a mile away, and eagerly offered assistance, then, indeed, his noble rage was a sight for the gods. "Assistance indeed! I suppose you think I don't know where I am. I suppose you fancy I have never been ashore in this craft before. I don't want much help from you to get off again on a rising tide, do I? I hope you will enjoy your row back again against the stream." The poor man was taken aback at his unkind reception, and sadly rowed home again to his ship.

The flats off Warden Point are so extensive that the best plan is to cheat the journey round them by cutting across, which can be managed, except near dead low-water time, if the boat does not draw more than three feet of water. It is as well to know that there are stakes here and there for fishing purposes, but only a few, so most people, I fancy, stand on over, and chance it—we do, and survive.

The shores off Warden Point are composed of mud and sand, the debris of the island of Sheppey, which is fast wasting away, being planed down by the sea to an uniform level, about three feet below low-water mark. We landed there once from the *Teal* to try and get some of the fossils, which are said to occur there in abundance, fruits of palms, and other signs of an ancient tropical vegetation which flourished in the basin of the Thames long ago, when the cheerful pterodactyl and the laughing hyaena had it all to themselves along the banks of the river, which was then many times larger than it is now. However, we did not bring away very much, probably through not knowing the things by sight; but having secured a bucket full of odds and ends, crystals of sulphate of lime, lumps of pyrites and other things, which looked as though they would do nicely for letter weights, we ended by forgetting all about them, and left them on the counter of the boat at Leigh, where they were no doubt found by the faithful, but unscientific Benson, and hove overboard to grace the mud on the Essex side for a change.

This visit called up memories of a former voyage to Warden Point, on a nasty squally day, in the little iron-keel boat of our friend F., a voyage which became matter of history at Leigh, because our safe return home the same day was so entirely unexpected by our friends there. We had gone down to Leigh the night before, and had turned in early, full of keenness for an early start next morning. We started off in good time, and ran down easily to Warden Point, and there landed, for no particular purpose except because we had set our hearts upon doing so, the wind freshening all the time from the westward, and it grew very squally and nasty as we were having lunch. F. was very fond of carrying his guests on shore, because it seemed to justify a certain outlay of his of several pounds upon a pair of boots of rubber and leather, which reached to his hips; having carried us ashore safely, he carried us back again, and then at last we began to wonder how we were to get home, for the weather was bad, and neither of his guests knew anything at all about the art of sailing a boat; in fact, we, like many other landsmen, thought the main sheet was the same thing as the main sail, but whenever F. ventured to throw out hints of the difficulty and danger of the return, we at once, in the most cheerful man- ner, said that we had every confidence in him, and that we left it entirely in his hands. However, having tied down two reefs and made snug, we took our stations and started off. To one of us was entrusted the duty of brailing up the mainsail when we wore ship, and the other was to manage the jib sheets. To tack the little boat was out of the question in the hollow sea. F. had the tiller and mainsheet. So we jogged along, cheerful though dripping with water, which came over the bows with every wave, working with what little shelter could be found under the island, and speculating upon our prospects when it should come to the time for crossing the channel to the Essex shore, for there were great rollers, as they seemed to us, out there in the middle. However, after a long and careful beat to windward, sailing the boat with all our might, that means, for our part, hauling on the brail rope and jib sheets frantically when ordered to do so, and looking with great awe and wonderment at the masterly seamanship of our skipper, we got up abreast of Cheney Rock, and the wind moderating, we ventured across all right; and by-and-bye, after a few thunder-squalls, the breeze came up from the eastward when we were off Southend Pier, and we sailed home as we had started, with a fair wind, shaking out the reefs, and setting the big jib for the run in.

We are not able to give any information about the anchorage off Whitstable, as we have never brought up there, but Speed, in his admirable book, *Cruises in Small Yachts*, and McMullen, *Cruise of the Procyon*, say that there is good anchorage on both sides of the Whitstable street, in six foot at low water time. Still, unless one is specially desirous of being at Whitstable, it is much better to go into the Swale, for the sake of peace and quiet, and a good night's rest.

In an exposed anchorage, where one is more or less on the *qui vive* for what may befall, and where the little boat rolls and tumbles all night long, sleep, if it comes at all, is a poor mockery of the real thing as enjoyed in a still, landlocked creek, safe out of the way of passing craft; and on a small vessel, even at the best of times, one's rest is liable to be disturbed by the novelty of the situation, and the various incidents of a night afloat, especially when one is only away for a couple of nights at a time, and has not had time to get used to the change. So it is of the utmost importance to take all possible precautions against needless disturbances by night, and to free one's mind from all anxieties about the vessel, for example, by having an anchor which can be thoroughly relied on for holding, and a riding light which can be trusted to burn all night. Be sure, too, that you know exactly what water you will have at high water time, and pay out the proper quantity of chain. Frap the fore haulyards round the mast to keep the ropes from flapping against it if a breeze springs up; give her a proper sheer to keep her steady to her anchor, and to prevent the rudder from bumping. Get the Berthon dinghy made snug, and so disposed that she won't keep knocking up against you all night (not always so easy a matter), and pack up the crockery so that it won't go adrift if she should roll when the tide turns. If you are in an exposed situation (which is to be avoided by all means in your power), see that everything is ready to hand for a possible start in the night under small canvas; then, having seen to all these points, and pumped her out dry, if need be, there will come to you that repose of mind without which there can be no repose of body, and the dawn will find you ready once more for the "Yo, heave ho!" with a cheerful countenance.

As we are in a moralising vein, I would further say that it is not always wise to take too much heed of the unsolicited advice which wise-looking old salts may offer; they will tell you that you can't fetch here or that you won't stem the tide there, or that there is or is not plenty of water in a given place, without knowing anything about the capabilities of your craft or of yourself, and without even knowing your draught of water.

I do not say that they are to be disregarded altogether, for their information is often most useful; but their facts are more valuable than their opinions, and what they say should be accepted, not as an oracle which cannot err, but as a contribution towards your stock of knowledge on the subject, to be weighed along with the rest of the information from other sources which you may happen to possess.

CHAPTER VI

The Swin Channel ~ The Buxey
The River Blackwater ~ Maldon
The River Roach ~ Havengore Creek

AFTER A TIME WE BEGAN TO GROW TIRED of the Medway and Swale, and began to look round for some more ambitious cruises. The Kentish coast did not seem very inviting. At Margate there was no decent shelter, and the other places on that side were no better, so we turned our eyes to the Essex shore. The Swin Channel was formidable, but the partner said he knew the way down, and that it was all right, and that he was game to tackle it; so at Whitsuntide, when the days were long, we made preparations and engaged a third hand, in the shape of a passenger. A handy man he was, and at once endeared himself to us by his fondness for cooking; a man who says he can cook is worth anything on a small boat. Most people at once say they can't, which means, at any rate, that they would rather not.

Men who come for a cruise are a quaint lot. Some come in their best clothes, but they soon learn that that is not a good plan; others go into the cabin and sleep all the time the boat is making a passage. This in itself is not a bad idea; I sometimes think I should like to be the passenger, and sleep in the cabin all the time, for the monotonous plash and tumble of the boat in a sea soon makes one feel like going to sleep. There was one friend of ours who went for a cruise in the *Teal* to the Norfolk Broads. He used to go ashore at night and sleep in hotels, whenever hotels were available, and he would turn up next morning pretending he had lost himself in the dark, and could not find his way back to the boat. He has never slept on board a small boat since that cruise, and he vows he never will. But that, if I may venture to use the expression, "is another story." To return to our cruise. We went on board in the evening, and dropped down with the ebb to Leigh Swatch, anchoring just inside the end of the pier, near the Leigh Spit buoy, in six foot at low water, and turned in early to be ready for a start at four the next morning. There was some plaintive person on the pier vainly hailing a craft for about half the night, as it seemed to us, but at last he gave it up, or, at any rate, we all got to sleep, and were awakened soon after sunrise by the voice of our captain. The partner was to be captain that morning, and we were to be common sailors, and do as we were bid. We had established a rigid rule that the man at the tiller was captain for the time being, and must be absolutely obeyed by the others, even if his orders seemed certain to lead to disaster; further, he was to be obeyed without any arguments from the crew. In this way the difficulties of the dual ownership were much simplified. "Now then, you common sailors, rouse and bitt, put the kettle on, and then make sail; fine morning, hi-i-i-h." We roused and bitted accordingly; all thought we'd have our swim by-and-bye, when the sun had aired things a little more. There were still two hours before high water, and, with a light easterly air, we just squeezed round the pier against the flood, and then made a long leg in over the flats to be out of the way of the tide. We worked along the shore and cooked breakfast, and had a bathe. We reached Shoeburyness at high water, and then stood off into the channel, and the wind coming up a little more southerly, we got the spinnaker out and were fairly off down Swin with the whole of the ebb under us, but not very much wind; it looked as though we were doomed to a day in the Swin Channel, but gradually we went along past the Maplin buoys, the Mouse Light-ship, and the Maplin Light, where formerly The Horns used to stand; a few old sailors still call the Maplin by the name of The Horns, and this part of the Swin is still called "Shoe Hole." Then our captain, with pride, pointed out the Swin Middle Light vessel; it was a great day for the novices, and we felt we were learning a lot, as we looked up the chart and saw the Barrow Buoys, and the Whitaker Beacon, and the Whitaker Spit Buoy, while the land was far away almost out of sight. The tide just carried us down to the Spitway Bell Buoy, and once through there, the flood would be in our favour for either the Colne or the Blackwater.

The end of the Whitaker Spit is a lonely kind of place, especially on a cold, grey day; it forms a sort of half-way house in going or coming between the Thames and the rivers Crouch or Blackwater, either at the end of a long thrash to windward, or at the beginning of one, for it is a long way from home for a small boat when the weather is not very fine. The beacon stands on the end of the Maplin Sand, which here runs out for seven miles from Foulness Point. The whole of the gulf round from Clacton to Brightlingsea, Burnham and the Whitaker is a sort of unshapen land, or rather a kind of wash, with that wicked Buxey Sand lurking in it, ready to pick one up in a moment if one gets out of the proper course; and that is not difficult, for the land is low and far away, and the buoys are at long distances apart, and the weather is seldom very fine and clear; besides the Buxey, there are the Swallow-tail, the Ray Sand, the Bachelor Spit, the Eagle, and the Knowl, all ready to catch one tripping. The hand-book says that the Whitaker Beacon stands in four foot of water, but we would advise no one to trust too confidently to that, for our own opinion is that there is a good deal less water there, and that it is very risky to cut across inside of it, except when the tide has flowed for an hour or so. The following adventure gives an instance of the difficulty of picking up one's marks in this part of the world. I was cruising one summer with a friend, and, on this particular occasion, was more or less acting as pilot. We had turned her down all the way from off Faversham Creek, against a northeast wind, and reached the Swin Middle Lightship at low water. The breeze was fresh, and we had come along capitally with the ebb. Somewhere off the Maplin Light we overtook and passed a big ketch, bound north. Our owner meant business that day, and was holding on to his big jib like grim death, although we were getting green water into it pretty often, and the crew, resigned to the chances of a ducking, was standing by all ready to jump forward to clear away the wreck, in case the head gear carried away. However, fate was kind, and the jib and jib-sheet and bowsprit all held. As we passed the ketch, her old skipper came to the weather rail to have a good look at us, and then set his foretop-sail, taking heart, we guessed, at seeing us go past him to windward in a little three-tonner, under all sail. Well, when we had reached the Swin Middle Light, the flood began to make up hard against us, and the end of it was that we could not weather the Whitaker Beacon, and had to make a few boards off and on, and then stand her over the sand inside it. There was a nasty sea

Down the Swin Channel

over the flat as we went across, not without some anxiety, but the lead gave us our water all the time, and only one of the breakers managed to get aboard, and that not badly, and soon we were over it, and heading for the Swallow-tail Buoy, and in the fair way for Burnham. Then we began to ask ourselves where was the entrance to the Burnham River? We saw some trees on the horizon, looking as if they grew out of the water, and we steered for them, thinking they were on Foulness Point, but soon found ourselves shoaling, and, at last, touched the ground. What was the matter? Were we too far to the southward, and on the Maplin, or were we too far north, and on the Buxey? We felt all at once as if we had totally lost our way, and, anchoring quickly, we pulled out the compass, and took the bearings of the lightship and the South Buxey Buoy and the Whitaker Beacon. That soon told us what was wrong. We had been heading for the Maldon River by mistake, and the course steered had been right across the Buxey, which naturally took us up before we had gone very far, and then, our eyes being opened, we discovered that our friend, the Buxey Beacon, was staring us in the face right ahead. Luckily, it was a flowing tide, and we were on the lee side of the sand, so no harm was done, and we steered a compass course until we made out the entrance to the Burnham River. That was a lesson in the use of the compass, and convinced us that it is not safe to go down Swin without one.

The *Teal* has had more strong winds in the channels round the Buxey than on all her other cruises put together. Once, going up to Burnham she had a strong westerly wind, bringing her down to smallest jib and close reefed mainsail, and close reefs meant a good deal in the snug old *Teal*. Again, she met very bad weather one Easter time in the Ray Sand Channel, both going out and when homeward bound, and twice had nasty weather going up the Maldon River, and another time she carried away her weather bowsprit shroud, and swamped her Berthon dinghy coming out of Burnham; a regular record of strong winds and rough water, so that we view the Buxey Sand, and all this part of the coast with a considerable deal of respect.

But to continue. We had safely negociated the spit way, and passed the Bell Buoy, and hauling our wind stood for the Knowl Buoy by compass course, and with the help of the passenger's opera glass soon picked it up. That glass was a treasured instrument, for there clung to it a faint and delicate perfume of patchouli, and it was passed around as a nervine stimulant when the crew and passengers of the *Teal* felt weary of the salt sea, for it called up memories of the pleasures of the land, the music and the dance, and what Mr. Mallock would call the "frou-frou" of the petticoat, what time the valiant skipper and his men disport themselves in modern Babylon. The passenger dare not come on board without it, for he knows full well that reproaches would be heaped upon him if he did.

We brought her to the wind off the entrance to the Blackwater River, and again had a swim and some food, and then letting draw foresail, off we went again for Maldon. There was a little fleet of oyster-dredgers pottering about, mostly belonging to West Mersea, and the wind freshening we shifted jibs and just lay our course up the Blackwater; we kept a look-out for the entrance to Bradwell Quay, but there was no time to go and look at it, and soon we were pelting along in the bright sunshine, and with a fresh southwest breeze humming in the rigging; past tempting-looking little creeks, with the masts of fishing craft at anchor inside them, offering no end of little corners for future cruises. The water was as clear as crystal; "on either side the river did lie long fields of barley and of rye," and patches of yellow and of crimson, where the mustard fields and clover fields were in blossom. Before reaching Osea Island, we noticed a bay on the southern shore which looked sheltered from westerly winds, and marked it down as a possible anchorage for the night. There was a coastguard station close by. Off Osea Island there was a smart Norwegian barque at anchor. The tide had been flowing for four hours by this time, and we went along all right until, on the spit which tails off from Northey Island, we ran upon the mud, but luckily did not stay there, and seeing beacons to the northward, we steered for them, and rounded the point all right, and brought up just off the mouth of the canal. We had been to Heybridge before by land, and had taken a good look round, so we chose a good berth and hailed an old salt to put us ashore and look after the *Teal,* while we went for a walk into Maldon. He gave up his fishing, which did not look very profitable, and seemed surprised to hear we had come from Leigh. "Why," he said, "I know Leigh. I bought a boat from there some years ago" (from the wily Benson, as it turned out); "but I thought you belonged to the place by the way you came up and anchored." There was glory for us. The passenger then wanted tea, so nothing would do but to walk into Maldon and find some. So we trudged miles in our heavy sea-boots, wearing holes in our stockings, until we came to an inn, where they provided the tea we sought for. When we got back to the boat we debated what to do next, and as the sun was setting rather angrily, and we felt we were a long way from home, and as it was uncertain whether we should lie afloat all night at our anchorage at Heybridge, we thought it would be wise to run back again as far as the coastguard station below Osea, and anchor in the little bay, close in shore, for the night, so as to shorten the journey next day. We soon got past Osea Island and picked up a berth close in, and were glad to turn in and sleep a good sleep, as we had been under way from four in the morning till nearly nine at night. We were almost too tired to eat our suppers, and far too much so to turn out when she took the ground at low water for about an hour, although we all awoke as she began to heel over a little, and there was a sleepy chorus of "Here, I say, is this what you call a snug berth? Hang it all, the bilge will come up into my bunk, if this goes on." The Captain's bunk was on the upper side, and he did not fear the bilge water, so he lay low, and only hoped he would not roll out of his bunk, but the Fates were kind and she heeled no further, and soon the hollow ship was vibrating once more, like a huge violin, to the shock of some vigorous snores.

In going up to Maldon, as soon as Osea Island is reached, the channel runs narrow; before that, it is all clear, and one need only keep somewhere near the middle of the river; but after Osea, there are great flats on the north side—Osea Flats; and there is a long spit on the south side, running off from Northey Island. There are beacons, most of them on the north side of the channel. The shore of Northey is fairly steep, and that is the proper side; along the next reach, past Heybridge, keep in the middle, and when past the bend the channel, up to the town, is marked by buoys, little cans and cones, all very correct.

The Hythe, Maldon

It is rather an undertaking to stay at Maldon Hythe. To lie afloat is impossible, because there is only about two foot of water in the middle of the stream at low tide. The best plan is to go alongside the shore near high-water time, just above the primitive bathing shed. There is a sloping gravelly bank, and the boat can be made to take the ground snugly enough, with a list into the shore, and an anchor out in the middle to haul off by. If Mr. Ben Handley or his sons are at hand, they will show how to do it, and give every assistance. They have a little fleet of pleasure craft, sprit-sail boats painted white and green, and are usually on the spot when wanted. Mr. Handley, senior, is a delightful-looking old gentleman, a retired pilot, who can tell many a tale of the former greatness of Maldon, before the Great Eastern Railway came to cut away all the sea-borne trade of the place. We photographed him at sight, with a quite killing grey curl over each ear, and were afterwards conducted to his cottage, where he shewed us all the other photographs which wandering cameraists had done of him.

The bathing costume of Maldon, in some cases at least, is rather diaphanous. *Procul este profani.*

Maldon is a very pretty-looking town perched on a hill, and very much set off by the old red church, which stands close to the Hythe. We fancied that the inhabitants must be bold spirits, for we saw an elderly gentleman and his wife go for a sail together on the tide in a gunning punt, much to the dismay of our country friend, the passenger. Maldon is an ancient place, and in the tenth century was infested by the Danes, who used to come freebooting, and there was a great fight there. They have left their names in several places round about this part of Essex, as in the place-names Danebury and Danesey Hundred, between the Crouch and the Blackwater. At the mouth of the Blackwater, near to Bradwell Quay, there was a strong naval station in Roman times, where the Admiral of the Fleet, or Count of the Saxon Shore, as he was called, had his head-quarters.

We left our anchorage early next morning, an hour or so before high water, with a strong westerly wind and cloudy sky, and the weather-going tide kicking up a hollow sea out in the middle, but it did not take us long to run down past Bradwell Quay and Pewit Island. We rounded St. Peter's Point, hauling our wind and keeping close in, as the tide was high and there was plenty of water. We could see the old chapel on the sea wall, and resolved to come by land some day and look at it, and see what was left of the Roman Admiral's villa. The *Teal* lay well down the Ray Sand Passage in a fathom of water, and, sounding at intervals as we went, we fetched to the Ray Beacon, and then began a long and salt turn to windward off the entrance of the Crouch, against the ebb. However, all things have an end, and at last we got into the river; and, by-and-bye, as we were nearing the junction of the River Roach with the Crouch, we espied a craft running down to us from Burnham, flying the Medway burgee, and with an all-new suit of canvas. "I say, Captain, I believe that must be the *Curlew*," said the skipper. "I wonder whether old Benson is on board?" We waved our hands, and could see that we were recognised; and as soon as she reached us, she rounded to, and came after us, but still there was no sign of Benson on board. We expected to be quickly overhauled by those new sails, but she only caught us up as we were going into the Roach River. "What cheer, *Curlew*. Are you cruising alone? Are you going out through Wakering Haven? Where's Benson?" "We are going to bring up directly, and wait for water."

"All right! so are we."

So we let go our anchor under the lee of the bank opposite the Coast-guard hulk *Lucifer*, to wait for water through the creeks, and then old Benson suddenly appeared from his hiding in the cabin, and hailed us. "Halloo, there! *Teal*, ahoy! Make way for a gentleman's yacht!" and steered straight for us. But we knew the old man's ways, and shewed no fear; and then he said he wanted us to throw him a line, to save himself the bother of letting go anchor, and weighing again; then there was more chaff. "I say, Benson, you nearly got took up at the point to the eastward there, coming into the Roach." "Not so near as you were, anyway; I see'd you pull your pole over, with only four foot; you had to put her round pretty sharp that time, I reckon. I said to myself, those chaps in the *Teal* will get ashore in a minute, and then we can go and laugh at them. I made sure you would, too; the water runs werry paltry just there."

"Ah, but don't you see, Benson, we 'knowed how to act within a little'"
(a favourite phrase of the old man's). "Are you going to stay in Havengore for
the night? You shall shew us how to do it."

This referred to instructions he had given us about the way of putting her
against the shelf at Havengore Creek entrance, so that the boat might lie on
the mud on an even keel all night. It turned out that Benson had guessed pretty correctly at our movements, and had timed his departure from Burnham
so as to join us, thinking we would go home through the creeks and stay the
night at Havengore, or Wakering Haven, as he always called it. So by-and-bye,
Benson, as Commodore of the Fleet, told us to make sail, and we started away
up the Roach, past the old Coastguard ship, *Lucifer*, through Devil's Reach,
where a squall came off the fields, and laid us down to the coamings, and into
the first channel to the left, among busy oyster craft and a superannuated old
paddle yacht, which was doing duty as a tug among a forest of oyster beacons,
and on through all the windings of the creek; passing by and noting the turn-
ings into Shelford and New England Creeks, and then going into Havengore.
There is a low "horse" just at the turn into Havengore Creek, but it has water
over it as soon as the rest of the distance is practicable. The oyster beacons
look quite bewildering at first, but they are really very useful. There is a double row on each side of the channel, standing upon the low part of the shore,
and behind them the sides rise up steeply. The tide flows in from the Crouch
nearly all the way, the highest part of the bed of the creek being right at the
mouth of Havengore, and the tide only comes in from over the Maplin during
the last quarter of the flood. The *Curlew* arrived first, having the best pilot,
and we followed, after grounding for a few minutes on the little hummock
nearly opposite the watch vessel. We were a trifle too soon, in fact, but had
the advantage of having the stream with us in the narrowest part; soon the
flood began to set in from the entrance, but we were snugly anchored by that
time, and had a swim, and a walk on shore, before making the final preparations for lying on the mud. At last the ebb began, and for a little while ran out
towards the Maplin, but by-and-bye it turned to ebb the other way, and the
boats swung round, and we took our anchors off on shore and trod them into

the bank, and then carried a line out from the masthead to the anchor, and poled the boat in till she grounded on the slope; then we hove the mast rope taut, to give her a slight list in, with bow pointing a little towards the land, and the deed was done.

The novelty of our position on the mud slope made us a little anxious lest something should go wrong in the middle of the night, and the romantic skipper was heard to softly murmur verses in his dreams. "All night no ruder air perplex Thy sliding keel till Phosphor bright Shall glimmer on our dewy decks." All was well, however, the keel did not slide, and next day we came out and home to Leigh without further adventure, but with the loss of much time in tacking against the ebb from Shoeburyness to Southend Pier. It did seem long that day, and we were glad to bring up at last in Leigh Swatch, and fish for flounders until there was water up the creek to Leigh.

CHAPTER VII
Through Havengore to Mersea Creek

A T FENCHURCH STREET STATION, one Saturday, just as we were starting for Leigh by the midday train, we found the owner of the *Curlew*, and on the way down we planned a cruise in company. Benson was coming in the *Curlew*, and we decided to make a trip round by Havengore Creek. So when Benson met us at Leigh Station he was at once assailed with questions. "Are the boats afloat yet? Have you got everything ready? Can we get into the Haven this tide?"

"That depends upon how soon you start; we may do it, if we make haste, but there is no time to be lost. The tide is high half-an-hour sooner there than here, and it's a good way beyond Shoebury. There's a nice breeze, so we shan't be so very long running down, once we start."

This seemed good enough, so we bundled headlong into the Ship Inn, and changed our respectability for old clothes and sea-boots; the skipper was ready first, so he went out for bread, eggs, and other supplies; and then we had some hurried lunch and made a start. Everything was soon put aboard, not forgetting a lot of well-brewed ginger-beer, which is the finest of mild alcoholic beverages, and off we went against the last drain of flood, speculating upon our chances of spending the night high and dry on the top of the Maplin, but having every confidence in Benson and his luck. We soon reeled off the miles to Southend Pier, and then steered straight for Shoeburyness Point, the *Curlew* leading; there we set spinnakers to save a little time, and at length we descried the mouth of Havengore Creek, with the flagstaff of the watch vessel inside. We could see the sand under us, green in the clear water, and not so very far underneath the keel either, and it seemed ever so long before the beacons off the entrance hove up in sight. We kept the pole going, but it gave us very slight comfort, and our hopes began to fall, for we had only a few inches to spare; however, we kept our eyes on the Commodore, and when he bore away to run down to the outermost of the beacons, we followed on; evidently we were not to sail straight into the creek over the top of the sands; at last he reached the lowest beacon and hauled his wind to try her in, and soon our water deepened too, as we got into the channel, and we braced sharp up, and just lay our course close hauled. Suddenly the *Curlew* stopped. "By Jove! they are ashore. What water have you?" The skipper kept sounding like a man with "Four feet, four feet, shoaling a little, shoaling, deeper, deeper, keep as she goes, we'll soon be up to them." Then came a stronger puff, and the *Curlew* heeled over, and on she went. "Hooray! They are off again. Good business." Ah-h-h! Our turn, and we stuck fast. We had been hugging the weather side of the creek a little too affectionately. "I'll get over," sang out the skipper, and in two two's he was in the water; then another puff came, and we began to move again. "Good, don't hug the weather side so much, we can lie through without squeezing, and I'll keep her from going to leeward. Don't forget the point, mind." "All right, one good luff up into the wind and in you get. The *Curlew* is in all right." With this we shot up into the wind, and then, bearing away, we were inside; great waving of hands from both craft.

"I say, I trod on a sardine tin, or something very sharp," said the skipper, "and I've cut my toe to bits." "Never mind, we have scored this time, and we shan't sleep on the Maplin to-night, anyhow."

Quickly we passed the Coastguard ship and came to the first fork, and then we had the stream with us.

"Look out for that point, the stream will set you on, if you are not jolly careful. I've slept there once and don't want to do it any more." "Oh, yes; I know who put her there, eh? after we had towed you up all the way from the entrance, with our sea-boots full of water, and all the spare line on board knotted together for a tow-rope—garn wi' ye."

So we slipped along with wind and tide, the creeks bank full.

"I say, this beats those feeble Broads, doesn't it?" said the passenger.

"You bet."

All was quiet and peaceful inside, the creek nearly bank full, with the oyster-boats swinging lazily at their anchors. Only a dog to bark at us from a boat in the Roach, as it was Saturday afternoon, and the oyster men had all gone home. Soon we were rounding to opposite the *Lucifer*, and going alongside the *Curlew* to make fast, as she had brought up before us. Then followed the stowing of the canvas, the singing of the kettle, the pipe, the riding light, the story, and the gentle plash of the water against the bows. Benson told us some amusing stories of our old friend F., and his goings on at Leigh. There was an old man there who kept a little inn, and in his parlour he had a stuffed bird, which had been brought home from foreign parts by his son, who was a sailor. This bird belonged to a genus which does not occur in Great Britain; and many had been the attempts to give it a name, but none were satisfactory to the old landlord, and he had gradually arrived at the belief that nobody on earth could know what bird it was. So F. used to have a go at the old gentle-man from time to time, and say, "I know what that bird of yours is, Mr. Wick-ens; why, of course, it is a Cape pigeon." "No, sir, it ain't, it ain't no Cape pigeon." "Well, then, it's a Mollyhawk, I am sure." "No, that it isn't! And what's more, sir, whatever you say it is it isn't! That's a bird unknowen."

One day F. and some of his friends had chartered Benson's little bawley, the *Emma*, for a day's cruise, and had taken their luncheon. By-and-bye they hove to somewhere near the West Ooze Buoy and began to feed; some hard boiled eggs were produced, and one fell into the hands of Benson's lad, who was with them. He turned it over and over, and when at last he got an oppor-tunity, he quietly nudged old Benson, and whispered to him, "I say, how d'ye eat these here things?" By-and-bye Benson's own turn came. We called out, "Benson, have some cherry brandy." At first the old man was doubtful, but at last he decided to venture, and tasted it. The flavour seemed to suit, for he handed back the empty glass remarking. "That's good, that is; I think I could take a drop of that almost any time."

We dropped astern to our own anchor before turning in, and early next morning came a bump, and I pushed out my head. It was just dawn, with a soft rain. A smart topsail trawler was hove to abreast of us, and the bump came from her dinghy, which was alongside.

"Would you like a nice sole, sir, this morning?" said Father Neptune in the shape of a fisherman, his beard dripping with the wet.

"Yes, let's have a look." And he held up some beauties, and we bought two, and told him to call next door. There they did not deal, however, and soon the trawler vanished again into the mist and rain. After that there was no more sleep, so we had a general rouse and tumble and a swim, and fried the soles and devoured them; and it cleared up and we decided to go to Mersea, and we were soon under weigh, with a light westerly breeze, keeping close together and chaffing old Benson.

The usual cormorant was sitting on the Ray Beacon, looking like a black wine-bottle, and in due course we were off West Mersea at the entrance to the Blackwater, and we stood in towards Mersea Creek, just scraping over the extensive flat which lies outside. Having got safely into the mouth of the creek, we ran ashore instantly on the opposite side of it. The bottom was of very soft clay, and was covered with long water-grass (*Zostera*), and the water was most beautifully clear, as compared with the turbid liquid found in the Thames, and we could see just under the boat's bottom a long broad furrow where some large craft had ploughed her keel through it. There are two ways into West Mersea, with a little island of saltings between them; we had taken the most northerly and narrowest of the two. We decided—easy decision as we were hard and fast aground—to wait for more water, so dropped the hook over and began our lunch, and the *Curlew* came up and joined us. While we were busy in this way a small fishing boat passed us, going in, so we indulged in a brief conversation with the skipper, who asked us if we were going into the creek. We said we were, and ventured the opinion that in his creek the channel ran rather narrow, and he, with a most supernatural and elfin sort of laugh, which haunts us still, agreed that it was "a bit orkard for strangers." While we were there, several more fishing boats went in, and we watched them to see how to do it. They sailed their craft full, getting as much way on as possible, and having a hand forward to tend head sails, and they hustled the boat round in stays as fast as ever they

could, for the channel was barely three boats' lengths wide; by adopting their plan, we by-and-bye got in, and anchored in mid-channel just above the boats, and then sheered over to one side to make room for passing craft, and with care and attention we were able to lie afloat all night in the tiny runlet which remained at low water. We went ashore in sea-boots, through the soft clay, and looked at the church and the village, and walked along the shore to try and find the *Pandora*, the hulk immortalised in *Mehalah* as the residence of Mrs. De Witt, alongside of Mersea Hard; but, alas, we could see no trace of it, but found that the creek turned to the northward, and grew broader inside, with an open reach and a flat sandy shore. Those who have read Mr. Baring Gould's novel would find all this region very interesting, and we resolved to seize an early opportunity of going up the creek to Salcott and Virley, where, it will be remembered, the wedding of Elijah Rebow and Mehalah was celebrated. Those who have not read the book are advised to do so, if only for the description of the ceremony and of the wedding breakfast which followed.

The view from West Mersea, looking south over the gulf of the Blackwater, is very pretty. The village stands upon a hill, and this is not unimportant, for on the Essex coast hills are scarce close to the water-side. The sunny slope, with the village and the church, at once took the fancy of the passenger, and he vowed that when he retired from the struggle of busy life (when he "cracked up," was his way of putting it), he would buy a piece of ground on the hill, and build a cottage and live happily, far from the smoke and strife of town life, but we told him to shut up. He always talks like that wherever he goes; but we know better, for he is wedded to the gas-lamps and the pavements, and would be bored to death in ten days anywhere out of London. Next morning we left Mersea at daybreak, and nothing would please the skipper but that we must run in behind Pewit Island to Bradwell Quay, just opposite, before starting for home, as it was high water and the opportunity might not occur again for some time; so we gave in and went over, and sailed in through a narrow entrance, between a little can buoy on the eastern edge and another buoy on the western, and went through and came out the other end, thankful to have escaped from the quicksands which surround the western part of

Pewit Island, and then came home by the Wallet Spitway, the Whitaker, and the Swin Channel. Bradwell Quay goes dry at low water, except just at the entrance, and is rather a doleful spot; still it might be useful to know of in bad weather; the western entrance is amongst endless mud flats, and is not at all easy to find, but the eastern is all right, and there is a homely and comfortable inn not far from the landing place.

The Wallet Spitway, between the Buxey and the Gunfleet, is said to be growing up very much. Commander Tizard, R.N., in a very interesting article on the Sands and Channels of the Thames Estuary, which appeared in *Nature* of April 10th, 1890, says that in 1800 there was a depth of nine feet best water in the Spitway, but that it has been steadily growing shoaler since then, until at the time of writing there was only five feet there.

CHAPTER VIII

A Night on the Maplin
The River Crouch ~ Burnham

I N ONE OF OUR EXPEDITIONS WE WERE BECALMED when half way down the Swin; and this proved the beginning of an adventurous night. We went away from Leigh in the afternoon, soon after mid-day, taking the ebb down, but off Shoeburyness the wind began to fall light, and the sail became a mere drifting match. It was at the end of May, and the weather was very fine and settled, and consequently the wind died down towards evening, as is so often the case in fine, summer weather; and so when we found that the ebb was done, and that the flood would soon begin to make up against us, we had to consider the position, and settle what we had better do. After discussing the advantages of waiting for high water, and then going in to Havengore at two in the morning, we rejected that plan and thought of another, which was to anchor on the edge of the sand and sleep until nearly high water, and then to cross into the Burnham River, over the high part of Foulness Sand. This idea seemed novel and attractive, so we rowed and poled her well inside of the buoys, on to the edge of the Maplin till we grounded, so as to be out of the way of all the traffic. We had supper, and after that the passenger was seized with a longing to go and potter about on the sand, so off he started in the Berthon dinghy, and paddled about with bare feet on the edge of the tide. By-and-bye, he came back with two huge whelks, which he had found walking about in the shallow water, having captured them after a great struggle, apparently, for he told us they were very strong; and, with true savage instinct, he at once set to work to boil and eat them, although he had only just finished a substantial meal. The captives of his bow and spear were accordingly boiled, and one was eaten by him, and the other was offered to the crew, but the offering was not received with much enthusiasm.

The Captain thought he would try his portion cold for breakfast, and it was accordingly put away carefully for him; but, when morning came, the gruesome object was hardly a tempting morsel, and was hastily thrown overboard. We then turned in, and so fine was it that we left the mainsail standing, and all went to sleep. At ten o'clock the skipper turned out for a look round, and stowed the sail, as there was a light breeze, just enough to make it fidget about. The moon was up; there was a haze covering the face of nature; and the green eye of the Mouse Lightship was blinking serenely through the mist. At eleven, a general wakefulness prevailed, and all hands were called. There was a light southerly draught of air when we made sail. The passenger appeared in a wonderful leather coat, black and shiny, "the skinny side out and the hairy side in," the latter being represented by a gorgeous red-flannel lining. We drifted, and sailed, and rowed through the mist, keeping the moon astern of us as best we could, though to do even that was not quite easy, for with so light a draught of wind and no landmarks, we found the stern of the boat trying to point in every direction but the right one. However, we persevered; the Mouse Light soon faded away out of sight, and we were in the middle of a great unknown. Still the Captain uttered words of wisdom. "If we only steer a little west of north, and keep at it, we are sure to hit Foulness Island in time; so we must just go on till we do so." At last we got into shoaler water, and were able to pole her along, one on each side; when the water shoaled too much we kept off a little more, and, after a long time, we began to hear a noise of water rippling against the bank, and soon we thought we could dimly make out the shelf at the point of Foulness. "Now then, you fellows," said the skipper, "we must buckle to, or we shall get left here for twelve hours; the tide must have begun to turn, and we are just on the highest part of the sand, with a bare three foot of water under us. There's a light away on the starboard beam, revolving; it must be the Swin Middle." "And what's that other bright light, right ahead? Oh, I expect that must be a barge, brought up in the Burnham Channel. We shall have her for company when we get over."

"By Jove, I feel half dead," said the passenger. "Where's the ginger-beer? Here, take hold of my oar while I broach a bottle."

"Very good, serve it out. I'll have one, too."

"And so will I."

Then three corks popped in the stillness, and three bottles gurgled out their contents; and we set to afresh with a will.

"Do you think we're deepening, skipper? "

"Not much yet. Go on like mad, or we shall get left here. Now I think we are better. Yes, deeper: much deeper."

"Now, passenger, get the topsail yard; and as soon as you can't touch bottom with it, sing out. I'll go forrard and get the anchor ready. When there's no bottom with the topsail yard we shall be all right at low water."

By this time we could feel the influence of the ebb out of the Crouch, and we could see, by watching the barge's riding-light, that we were drifting down with it, and soon the passenger sang out, "Let go; no bottom." And the chain rattled merrily out into about four fathoms of water, and in a very short time sails were stowed, and all turned in.

"I say, how long do you think we've been at this little game?"

"I've no idea; all I know is, I am jolly tired of it."

"Well, it's three o'clock; so we have taken four hours. Don't forget to wind up watches, all hands. Good night! Tie up the riding light before you come below."

"Ay, ay, sir."

At seven, I looked out; it was nearly low water. The day was raw and wet, with an unpleasant, greasy sort of southerly wind blowing; so I put on sea-boots and top coat, and said we ought to shift, and go into the river. The passenger was told off to boil the kettle, because he said he felt cold, and we hoisted jib and mainsail, and pottered along into Burnham. The barge was still asleep, about a mile off to the northward of us, with her riding light still showing a glimmer. It soon grew warmer and finer, and when we came to Burnham, we all thought it a good opportunity to go on with the tide as far as we could up the Crouch, and come back to Burnham with the ebb in the afternoon. It turned out a blazing hot day after all, and we went miles up country, through long, straight reaches, with a ferry here and there, past Cricksea, where there was a lovely forty-ton yawl, lying at a mooring just off the end of her owner's garden, which provoked much envy; past Bridgemarsh Island, with a fleet of little oyster boats snugly anchored in the creek; past Fambridge, until we came to a place where the river divided, part going straight on and part turning to the southward. We had sailed out of the chart before this, but there was a land map of Essex on board, which told us the left-hand turn was the main channel. Whereupon, from a spirit of contrariness, we took the other way, and, by-and-bye, we cast anchor in a field, and went for a walk on shore. We had got to a place called Salt-Coats in the map, and could go no further; but that did not matter, so we swam and lunched and smoked until the tide turned and it was time to go back. We had come about fifteen miles up from Foulness Point, and enjoyed ourselves much; especially at the novelty of being able to put the anchor in a field. On the way back to Burnham we all grew more or less torpid from the heat, taking turns to steer and to sleep. The steersman constructed a penthouse for his head against the sun with a copy of the *Field* newspaper, and the others lolled about the boat semi-comatose, and insisting on a perpetual thirst. We were to stay at Burnham for the night, and we had to choose an anchorage. Out in the middle the tide runs very strongly, and the bottom of hard clay is not very good holding ground, because it is scraped smooth by continual oyster dredgers, and an anchor may not bite properly. At least, we dragged our anchor there one night, and only by a lucky chance managed to keep clear of the numerous dredger boats which take up nearly all the room opposite the town. Then there are the oyster beds, which must not be forgotten. Oyster is king in Burnham, and if they see a boat anchor too near the edge, a man will be sure to come off in a few minutes to request the boat to shift, for fear of grounding on the oysters. The most convenient places for a little craft are in the bight just off the upper part of the town, but not too near the shore, for reasons given, or just below the Watch Vessel, again not too near the side. The fishing boats lie at anchor so thick opposite Burnham that it is a trying matter to tack through the fleet; from a little distance off it looks almost as hopeless as having to

tack through a wood. However, it has to be done, so one must plunge boldly
in among them, and trust to luck and attention, standing by for a tack, or
else a fisherman's half-tack, at a moment's notice.

The oyster companies have watch towers in the town of Burnham,
whence they can look out and survey all the windings of the Roach, and
they keep a swift cutter on the grounds to pursue suspicious-looking strangers. The cultivation of oysters is full of mystery to the uninitiated, one
of the chief duties of the people apparently being to dredge them up from
one place and throw them back again in another; perhaps the oyster loves
change of scene. They also harrow the bed of the river before laying down
the oysters. Hundreds of tons of oysters are imported by steamer from
Bordeaux, and laid down in these creeks, where they quickly improve and
fatten, and become quite unlike the skinny bivalve that one sees in French
towns. Salmon, in his *History and Antiquities of Essex*, 1740, says, "Here
is an excellent nursery for oysters, which are brought hither small, and
spread about from a shovel till they come to their proper growth," and he
adds, as a valuable contribution to their natural history, that "it is observ-
able that those which lie with the concave side uppermost thrive as well
as the rest, which lie in what we think their proper posture." Once when
we were spending a quiet day in the Creeks we made friends with the
men on the watch boat, and were invited on board to see their vessel. She
had a capital cabin, and was very well built and fitted. Her builder was a
carpenter at Paglesham, of great renown as a builder of these pretty and
graceful oyster craft. We also took a walk on shore, and saw the oyster
ponds which they dig on the saltings, just at the level of high tides, and
it was a sight to make the mouth water to see oysters lying there in hundreds in the clear water, within reach of one's hand, all ready for market.
In these creeks the Burnham oyster grows into a plump and luscious morsel, and we resolved to go ashore to the inn to dine, and have some to begin on. The oysters at Burnham are extremely fine, and to our taste they
are far superior to the Whitstable oysters. So we adjourned to the *White
Hart*, a very good inn on the water front of the town. A small boy put us

Burnham

ashore, and promised to look out for us later on and take us back, and we entrusted him with the riding light, and told him to put it up when it got dark. He examined the *Teal* minutely and with approval, especially when we put her under his charge.

"Ah!" he said, "there was a fine yacht came up here last week; two masts she had, and a band of music aboard."

"Well, but Tommy, we've got two masts, haven't we? And how do you know we don't carry a band of music? You have not heard the passenger snore yet."

Tommy smiled, and gently put the question by. We bought some provisions for the ship, and had our meal on shore, and trotted back to the vessel in good time.

"Don't you forget, you fellows," said Pardner, "that we have to get home to Leigh to-morrow, and must be at the Whitaker by low-water time."

"All right; we'll turn out at six, if that will do."

"Well, I don't know so much about that; if there's an easterly wind it will take us a long time to get down. We can't run any risks. I think we ought to be off at five."

"All right; you call us. Good-night."

Five o'clock soon came round, and found us fast asleep; but it wasn't long before we were being reminded, in a doleful voice, of the distance to Leigh and the fickleness of the winds, and that old proverb about time and tide; and, as we objected to the "I told you so," which we knew would follow in case of any failure in the passage, we pulled ourselves together, and made our beds, and pretended to be all alive. The sails got set somehow, the anchor weighed in the same manner, and the good old *Teal* with her sleepy crew was wandering off again towards the mouth of the river, and the passenger was soon deep in the preparation of kippered herrings, *à la* Cruising Club, a masterpiece of his own invention.

"What's the use," he used to say, "of having to fool away at the skin of the kipper while you are eating it? Much better take away all skin and bone before cooking, and have it filleted in a proper manner."

Barge Crossing the Maplin

"Hear, hear," from the crew. "*Mucho bueno.* You *are* a good cook, passenger! We'll have them your way; your reputation as a *chef* is at stake. Keep her full, Capting."

"Ay, ay! just trim sail a bit, common sailor; confound you, your jib-halliards are not half set up. The jib-halliards are the first string of the violin; no music in going to windward if they are not taut; and your main and peak are all anyhow. How can I push her down to windward in this trim? They'll say she's got a crew of soldiers aboard, and you had better stow the chain in the locker, and wash decks while you are about it."

"Ay, ay, Capting; and after that, shall I fill and light your pipe for you?" the passenger then chirped in.

"Mutiny aboard, by the powers! There'll be hanging of someone at the yard-arm directly."

"Yes, or else we'll maroon the passenger on Foulness Point. I think he must have had too much cooking this morning; the fumes must have got into his head."

"I say, do you remember our going ashore on Foulness Island, and seeing that sheepfold? Jolly snug it was, with walls of fern and reeds, four feet thick, and kept out the east wind well, didn't it? "

"Yes, as warm as a greenhouse any day."

"Well, if we can only fetch the 'Wikerer' by low water, we shall be all right. I wouldn't stand in too much towards the Maplin, skipper; it runs out in shoals here and there. We stirred the sand up when running out along here once, and jolly nearly got left high and dry, too."

So we tacked along with a good ebb, and got down and round the beacon by slack-water time, then bore away joyfully for home, with an east wind which gave signs of freshening as the day warmed, and were soon slipping along the Swin, feeling quite at home among the goodly company of barques, barges, steamers and other craft which commonly infest the Swin Channel.

CHAPTER IX

To Burnham and Wivenhoe, through the Creeks

THE WINTER SESSION HAD DRAGGED its tedious length along, and a few signs of returning spring were beginning to shew themselves, when one Thursday before Easter I reached the platform at Fenchurch Street Station, laden with handbags, blankets, Brittany butter, chutney, and other necessaries of life, just in time to catch the 12.8 train for Leigh, and there discovered the partner buying newspapers and looking about anxiously for me. "Hillo! Captain," he cried (we always talk like that when we go sailing), "I thought you must have been took up on a bit of a spit, and were going to lose your train. Have you remembered that cherry-brandy, and the cawfee, and those other things we've heard so much about? I've brought a fine piece of cold beef, enough to last us a week, almost. And we mustn't forget the mint bullets for the medicine chest when we get to Leigh." The mint bullets are pepper-mints—bulls' eyes—of globular shape, black streaked with white, and of the strongest flavour, which are invariably carried with us on a cruise for their medicinal virtues, and to ward off the dyspepsia which is likely to arise when one is living on food of one's own cooking, because that inevitably leads to a reduction of the cookery to the lowest possible terms.

The *Teal* is victualled upon unusual, but, we venture to think, highly scientific lines. We both hate cooking, and so provide a large piece of good boiled beef as a *pièce de resistance*; we take lots of oranges and ginger-beer, for their anti-scorbutic qualities, and the mint bullets aforesaid for a medicine chest, and chutney, which is both condiment and sweetmeat, and then just fill up with some sausages or kippered herrings, and trust to renewals at the ports we may chance to reach; and when opportunity arises we seize it and dine ashore, highly enjoying the return to such a luxury as a clean table-cloth.

Cooking, and, what is worse, washing up of plates and dishes, is the burden which sooner or later wears out the endurance of the amateur crew; they gradually come to shirk the hateful business, and we have at last been forced to adopt a strict rule on the *Teal* that each shall wash up his own plates and mugs and knives and forks, as soon as he has done with them, and to this *modus vivendi* we manage to adhere. Cruising on a small boat soon teaches a man what are the actual necessities of life, and what are mere luxuries, and the latter are quickly discarded if they cost any trouble. Of course, all small-boat sailors are not of one mould. Some spend their time in holystoning the deck and scraping the chain cable, and care but little for sailing. Others, again, use their boat for fishing or for shooting, while others take their pleasure in sailing and making passages, and in getting fresh air and exercise. If one lives near the water and has plenty of spare time, it is possible to attend to all the small details of refitting, and to keep the boat very smart, and when we are old, and retire to live quietly in our sea-side cottages, with a flagstaff in the front garden, we will do so too; but when one hurries from London to snatch a holiday between Saturday and Monday it is imperative, if one means cruising at all, to hoist up sail as soon as one gets on board; even then half the holiday is consumed in getting from home, and the other half in getting back again in time to catch one's train. We have, therefore, been forced to leave everything in the way of fitting out to the somewhat casual Benson, although we might find any amount of delight in that side of yachting which includes scraping, varnishing and splicing, if there were time and leisure for it. A Leigh bawley man, who gave us a help into Leigh one evening up the creek, asked us: "Who fits you out? She looks a bit rough." "Why Benson; you know him, don't you?" "Yes; I thought she looked a bit in his style, with those old lanyards."

Well, we got down to Leigh and victualled the vessel, and put on board the beds, the fresh water, spirit for the stove, and paraffin for the riding light, and started off with a very light easterly air. The partner took first turn to be common sailor, and I took the tiller. We set the sails and let go the mooring, but after sitting aft for several minutes and working that tiller about, I began to think all was not right, for though answering her helm she did not go through the water at all; so I called out to Benson, who was rowing by after putting us on board, that she was not sailing very fast, and he replied: "Well, you ain't let go your mooring yet." The common sailor had dropped the mooring buoy

West Shoebury Buoy

overboard without looking after it, and it had gone foul of the bobstay, and was holding us. After getting clear we tacked down quietly to Southend Pier, bringing up inside the Leigh Spit Buoy in the lower part of Leigh Swatch. The partner then said he was going ashore, and did so, bringing back with him some more oranges and a tin to keep the coffee in, and a lobster; while we were going down a bawley went by with spinnaker set, and holes in his ragged old topsail. He greeted us and said we wanted more wind. So we told him his topsail didn't seem to want much more wind. He grasped our subtle meaning, but promptly explained that they were only "air 'oles."

We decided to go through the creeks next day, so after breakfast took the ebb down with a south-westerly wind, as far as the West Shoebury Buoy, searching for a gatway that we had been told to look for by Benson, which runs into the sand for a mile or more, and opens out into a lake-like basin, where one can lie afloat at low water, with sands all round. A place very well to know of, if one could be sure of finding it, in case of being becalmed in that part of the world on the ebb tide, or in any other way prevented from getting up to Southend for the night. When we got down to it there was the entrance plain enough, and boats inside, and people on the sand gathering cockles; so we stood in for the opening in the sands, but shoaled our water so fast to three feet that we did not like it, and hauled out again. There was a fresh breeze, and we were moving along rather too fast to care to take the ground, especially on a lee shore, so brought up just outside, wishing we could get in to the de-sired haven, but at dead low water the bar at the mouth seemed to have only about three feet best water, and we did not know the entrance very well, so anchored for an hour's flood. While we were waiting two light barges came in and plumped themselves at the entrance; they both stuck fast but kept their sails up, and with the wind aft the one nearest the middle of the channel slowly drove through it and anchored inside, and we could see her skipper get into his boat, and go for a walk on the sands; the other one was too much to the westward and stuck fast, so he hauled aft his mainsail and forced her off again, and made a little trip out, and then came back and went in successfully. A bawley, too, had arrived by this time, and brought up close to us, and the

Havengore Creek: The Entrance

hour soon passed, and having had a lead from the barges, we tried her in and found plenty of water, sounding with the boat-hook as we went over the bar, and having got in we brought up again.

This Swin Way is a good place to wait in before going in over the sands to Havengore; the stream of flood sets strongly through it, and over the Maplin from south-west to north-east, that is, in a direction opposite to that in the main channel, so that small craft, bound down, can get along with a fair tide over the Maplin, and if they draw only about three feet, can cut across the Whitaker Spit, and get into the Burnham River by the Ridge Buoy, at a place where the sand is low, thus saving a long round, and dodging a foul tide. There is another Swin Way of the same sort close at the back of the Maplin Lighthouse, where a boat drawing three feet can go in and find a fair tide on the flood to the same low way over the Whitaker. The only risk is a wreck on the Whitaker Spit, about two miles inside of the Whitaker Beacon, which is covered and hidden from sight at half-tide.

The tide made up very fast, and soon we weighed and started for Havengore over the sands, but the sight of a horse and cart crossing the entrance of the creek shewed us that we were too soon to get in; we therefore brought up again, and by-and-bye one of the light barges made a start and stood in under foresail and topsail. We watched her, and thought that we should do best with plenty of sail on, as the creek's mouth ran almost dead to windward for a short but critical part of the course, so we set the mainsail and jib, which had been hauled down while we were going over the sands and shoal water. The wind had been freshening all the morning, and there was a slashing breeze. We weighed anchor, having about four feet of water, where we were on the flat to windward of the creek, and bearing up we ran down to the beacons, sounding as we went with the boat-hook, ready to run her off if the water shoaled too much, and standing by to flatten in the sheets as soon as the water deepened, and we reached the creek. The old barge had got into the channel between the beacons all right, but having little way on, and no mainsail set, she was all the time sagging to leeward, and at last she stuck fast on the lee side of the channel, just on the point of the bend. Then our turn came; the water deepened as we slipped into the fair way, and sheeting home the sails smartly, we just clawed along through, though we barely had our water as we passed the spit, and there was the old barge's anchor sticking up out of the water a yard or two off; but we helped her along with vigorous shoves of the oar against the bottom. Once past that point we were able to bear up for a short distance, and could just lie along the first reach past the Coastguard vessel, and then kept away, going at a rattling pace, with sheets slacked, right along to the River Roach. For a long time we looked back and watched the barge hanging on the point, and pictured the crew still shoving and shouting, as they were revealed to us during the tremendous moment of our own lucky shoot past them, and rejoiced at our escape from drifting down there, too, with them. The entrance to the creek is very narrow, and is beaconed by posts. Those to the north are strong and high, those to the south are slight; the deepest water is midway between them. On the shore are two beacons like those marking the channel, but stouter; stand on boldly, until quite close to the first one, for the best wa-ter, as there is a spit opposite which is very treacherous, and runs out a long way, and the channel takes a curve round it; after passing these, keep in mid-channel. There is a small horse opposite the Coastguard hulk, but it is not im-portant. After passing the watch vessel the creek divides, with a considerable spit of mud on the point, and as the stream sets strongly inland from one hour before high water until low water, there is risk of getting on to it, especially in tacking, unless one is careful. The barge got to leeward through want of sail, and we should certainly have done so too, had we tried to get in under jib and mizen. After we had reached the Roach, we could see that the two barges and the bawley had succeeded in getting through all right at last.

Mr. Speed, in *Cruises in Small Yachts*, gives a capital account of these in-side channels, and a glance at a chart will shew that there are several islands to be circumnavigated by the curious explorer at high-water time.

The channels, which are bank full at high water, present at low water a very different appearance; their sides are extremely steep, and composed of soft mud; the water ebbs entirely away from the part between the entrance at Havengore and the point off Shelford and New England Creeks, but from there onwards to the Roach and Crouch one can lie afloat anywhere, care being taken not to take the ground on the edge of the cant, for fear of a headlong plunge at low water into the gulf beneath.

Scattered along the last reaches are the oyster boats, little carvel built craft of about six or seven tons, with remarkably yacht-like overhanging sterns, and having a peculiarly Dutch look when under sail, due partly to their short gaffs and long vanes, and partly to their being without topmasts, in place of which they have a small flagstaff only. They are wonderfully handy, and some of them have nice roomy cabins, as we know through having been aboard of one of a rather better style, which was used as a watch boat. Many of these vessels are built at Paglesham, on the River Roach, and a few at Burnham.

On reaching the River Roach it can be seen to run westwards towards a clump of trees, which mark the position of Paglesham, and eastwards, round a bend known as Devil's Reach, past a large Coastguard hulk, the *Lucifer*, to join the Crouch or Burnham River, about two miles below Burnham. We ran quickly through Devil's Reach, gybing over as we entered and again on leaving it, with a strong wind behind us, and began to make things snug and tidy below, in expectation of a wet thrash to windward up to Burnham. The flood was by this time done, but we hoped by the help of the strong wind, to stem the tide, which runs down in a most uncompromising manner between the straight banks of the river. As there are no headlands or slack waters, there is no possible chance of cheating it. Our first few tacks were very good ones, though rather wet in the hollow seas in mid-stream, but soon, the ebb making down strong, and the wind at the same time falling light, we found more sail was wanted, so hauled out the mizen and set the big jib, and at last, after many boards, succeeded in getting up to Burnham, and anchored below the Coastguard hulk, close to the edge of the mud, having just our water at dead low tide. Two Coastguard men were soon alongside, and undertook to put us ashore, and to take us back again, if we wished, later in the evening.

Burnham, as seen from the river, is a picturesque little place, with its red brick houses and its fleet of oyster dredgers; it subsists mainly upon its oyster fishery, and a little in the way of boat building. The 'pardner,' in a most de-

Oyster Boat, Burnham

generate way, insisted throughout this cruise on dining and sleeping ashore, regardless of the fact that this was hardly playing the game; and I joined him in decay so far as the dinner ashore was concerned, but preferred to sleep aboard, as it enabled me to change plates each evening in readiness for next day's photographing.

At dinner our spirit of enterprise began to assert itself once more, in spite of cold and wind, and we decided to go on next day to Wivenhoe, if there was anything like decent weather; so in the morning, at seven, I went to fetch the Skipper in the Berthon, taking his sea-boots along for him to wade through the mud with, and we were soon off with a fine breeze on starboard quarter, breakfasting under way. It was a grey and cloudy morning, and after leaving the river we began to peer out for the West Buxey Buoy, the Ray Sand Beacon and the Buxey Beacon. The West Buxey is on the south-west corner of the Buxey Sand, and marks the point between the Whitaker Channel and the Ray Sand Passage. It is the first buoy made on the outward passage from the Crouch, and the line from it to the Swallow-tail Buoy marks the north side of the Whitaker Channel, and the line from it to the Buxey Beacon and North Buxey Buoy marks the east side of the Ray Sand Passage. The distances from mark to mark are all rather long out here among the sands, and we ran along some little time before we made out the buoy, but having picked up both it and then the Buxey Beacon, we came to the conclusion that the Ray Beacon was *non est*. After coming up to the Buxey Beacon we stood nearly due north, sounding as we went, and expecting to find water over for us inside the Bachelor Spit, which would have shortened our passage a little, but the water shoaled in a way we did not like, and we hauled our wind abruptly and stood off into the channel, and there, under our lee, could distinctly see the highest part of the Bachelor, awash with breakers. We had very nearly put her ashore there, and but for the careful use of the sounding pole, and the Skipper's good look-out, we should have had her bumping on the hard sand a few minutes later; and there was enough sea on to make that a serious matter. The whole of the bay off the Mouths of the Crouch, Blackwater, and Colne is rather awkward and tiresome, demanding the utmost attention to soundings,

buoys, and general look-out; and as there is generally plenty of wind, and often a haze which makes it hard to see the buoys, the navigation of these parts
is difficult, and this makes it a good training ground. An acquaintance of ours
slept on the top of the Buxey one night in a three-tonner, feeling jolly anxious
as to the weather he was to have on the flood in the morning, and we have
ourselves had, in a calm, to row hard to avoid being set on to the south-west
edge of the same sand, by the ebb sweeping over it out of the Burnham River.
After getting back into the channel, we steered the proper course to the North
Buxey Buoy, and then to the Knowl, which serves as a mark for the entrance
to both Blackwater and Colne, and from there stood in to the mouth of the
Colne, keeping between the buoy on Bench Head and that on the Bar. The
wind was fresh and the sea was breaking over the Knowl as we went flying
past with second jib and main tack triced up; and when well inside the Colne,
and passing the entrance to Brightlingsea, we stowed mainsail, and went on
to Wivenhoe under jib and mizen at a fine rate. We shortened sail because the
Colne was almost strange to both of us, and for the same reason kept fairly in
the middle of the river, passing a big steam yacht, *Lady Torfrida*, which was at
anchor there, flying the same burgee as ourselves—the Medway Yacht Club,
to wit—and with the American ensign over her stern. We avoided the points
where spits seemed likely to be lurking, and kept her well over in the hollow
bights of the different reaches. We just scraped over the top of the shoal in the
reach below the bend into Wivenhoe, and rounded the little black buoy on the
spit which runs out so far at that point. When we got to Wivenhoe we took
up a berth near the Ferry Hard, but finding it rather inconvenient, we shifted
over to a buoy nearly opposite, where we were less beset by small urchins in
punts. There are lots of mooring buoys at Wivenhoe, made of huge chunks
of water-logged wood, rather unwieldy, but still convenient for strangers. We
changed our things and went on shore to look round, and see the yachts fitting
out, and I took the opportunity of sending off by post the photographic plates
which had been already exposed, for fear lest the sea air might be bad for their
highly delicate constitutions; and then we asked some yacht hands who were
loafing on the quay to tell us the name of the best hotel. They mentioned one

we had already looked at, and so we said it did not look much from an outside point of view, whereupon one of the three began to snarl and growl at us, saying it was "good enough for the dukes, earls and markisses wot came there," and how Lord So-and-so habitually used it, in preference to his own country house, until we mildly pointed out that we were ready to take his word that it might be all right within, and that he need not make such a fuss about it. We decided to try the inn in question, and found it first-rate inside. Moral: Don't always judge by exteriors. After a walk round the shore to see all the big yachts fitting out, we discovered a vessel we thought we knew, a barge-yacht, built by Gill, of Rochester, for winter shooting on the Norfolk Broads, and we held a parley with her genial and rotund skipper. She was a queer sort of a craft, like a huge box, but with any amount of cabin accommodation, judging again by exteriors; we noticed that she had discarded her sprit, and her skipper told us that it rolled about so in a sea way that they had been obliged to give it up, and have a gaff mainsail instead. He said she splashed about a lot in rough water, and wanted more canvas. We also saw a novel kind of dry dock there, made out of an old vessel's hull, and having a little steamer berthed snugly inside it.

We then went on to Rowhedge, where there are more yachts laid up, both old and new; and after dinner on shore we retired on board to sleep; we took the ground at our mooring for about an hour at low water, as the river runs nearly dry at that time; and next morning we made an early start soon after half ebb. It was an unpromising sort of day, cloudy, and looked like bad weather, so we jogged along under jib and mainsail, down the mouth of the river, and brought up under the weather shore of Mersea Island, opposite Brightlingsea, to wait and see how the day would turn out, and whether we could venture to try her back to Burnham, but it came on to blow so hard that at midday we had to run into Brightlingsea to wait for finer weather. There were three or four other yachts anchored near us, off Mersea Island, also waiting for better weather. The owner of one had his family on board, and by-and-bye the children all went ashore, in charge of one of the sailors, to run about and play, and we thought we couldn't do better than follow their example, as sailing was out of the question. This was Easter Sunday, and the little harbour at

Brightlingsea was crowded with yachts and craft of all sorts, and as we came in under jib and mizen we wondered where we should find a berth, but managed to pick a good one just inside by the ferry, close under the sand bank on the south side. This is the best place for holding ground, and it is more convenient for getting out again than any place further up the harbour. At the entrance to Brightlingsea, off the north shore, there is a long spit, conveniently marked when we entered by a barge aground on the point, and there is a mud flat opposite. There were lots of yachts in there that day, and all through the afternoon it blew harder and harder, so that we congratulated ourselves upon being safe in harbour, where we were well off, and were not trying to push her down to windward in the Ray Sand Channel, against the strong south-south-west wind; and it was fine fun to see the big yachts coming in or running up the Colne under small canvas, and to see how the crews of every yacht already inside were on the *qui vive* to see each new comer arrive; and how, when she was safe in and anchored, they once more all vanished below, out of the wind. A big North Sea dandy, from Grimsby, the *Protrude* (what a name!), came in and spent most of the afternoon in warping herself into a good berth, with ropes and anchors out in all directions; then a smack of about forty tons, with two fishermen and a party aboard, showed signs of making a start. As they lay quite close astern of us, with other vessels all round, we began to wonder how they would get out without going foul of something, for we lay close to the bank, and there was a biggish yacht, not far off, on our port quarter, and another on our starboard beam. However, with two reefs down, and spitfire jib set, they weighed anchor, and down they came towards us, their anchor only just off the ground, and two hands working frantically at the capstan, steering between us and the weather shore, where there was precious little room for them; we felt sure that their boom must go foul of our mizzen-mast, or that their anchor would pick up our chain, or that we should lose our bowsprit; but the man at the helm was on the watch, and sang out to his crowd to get in their mainsheet smartly, which they did only just in time to clear us, and soon she was beyond the shelter, and smashing out against wind and tide, with spindrift flying off like smoke all along her weather quarter.

The wind took off a good deal at sunset, but it was rather anxiously that we contemplated a tremendous westerly bank of clouds as we were turning in, for we wanted to make an early start next morning. However, the day broke beautifully fine, and the first to get out was a barge, laden with a haystack. We awoke just as she went slipping past us, in the grey of the morning, with her red sail gleaming in the early sun, and this was the signal for us to rouse and bitt, and we were very soon turning out in company with quite a fleet of fishing boats, all offering most tempting pictures for the camera. The crew of the *Teal,* however, were far too busy with making sail, stowing the Berthon in the cabin, coiling down spare warp, and cooking breakfast, and generally getting ready for a dusting outside, to think of snap-shot photography. Our thoughts were rather whether we should make our passage into the Crouch before it began to blow, as the mares' tails, interlaced all over the sky, threatened would be the case before the day was half over. However, with a nice south-south-west breeze, we tacked along past the Knowl Buoy into Swire Hole, and on by the North Buxey Buoy, into the Ray Sand Passage; judging it best not to try the Swin Channel, but to keep inside, and go home by the route we had followed on the outward journey. In the Ray Sand Passage we kept the lead going, and felt a glow of wicked satisfaction when we saw another little yacht, which had started from Brightlingsea with us, get ashore on the Ray Sand, just where it runs out flattest and farthest by the beacon, to stick there for an hour through neglect of the same precaution. Soon after getting into the Burnham River, there were some strong puffs from the southward, which gave us all we cared for under jib and mainsail, and when we neared the mouth of the Roach, we brought up under the weather shore for lunch, and to wait for water through the creeks, while a heavy squall came up and passed over. Up it grew, black as ink, with lightning and heavy rain, and hailstones; but we were in harbour, all snug under the weather shore, so could scramble below out of the rain, and peep out to enjoy the prospect, and see our consort catching it like fun out in the middle. By-and-bye, at half flood, we weighed again, and went on through the creeks to Havengore, with finer weather, doing the last mile in a heavy shower of hail and rain, but without much wind,

Smack Leaving Brightlingsea

and there we anchored against the shelf for the night. We had company that
evening, for a Bawley boat, belonging to Benfleet, arrived soon after us. They
had been with a cargo of cockleshells for the oyster grounds in the Roach,
and were on their way home again; and, in the morning, we both started away
together, and soon the *Teal* was once more trying to squeeze up Leigh Creek
against an ebb tide, with the usual result of sticking fast half way. Benson was
soon down on us, though; he was out rowing his punt in the creek with two
small boys, and spied us, and came down to welcome us back after our stormy
and squally, but capital cruise.

"Halloo, Benson, we couldn't manage the creek this time, you see; we
took the wrong turning, I think."

"Ah! I'm werry glad to see you safe home again, this squally weather.
Where were you yesterday, when that bad squall came over?"

"Oh ! we were all right. We had just got inside the Burnham River. Will
you take the *Teal* in next tide? We want to get home; we haven't had breakfast
yet, for we finished all our food last night." "All right, sir."

So we waded over the mud in our sea-boots, and were soon snugly anchored at the table of the Ship Inn, combining breakfast and luncheon in one
solid, square meal, before starting back to town.

CHAPTER X

The River Lea ~ Bow Creek
Stangate Creek ~ Lower Halstow ~ Upnor

HAVING SHIPPED AS CREW in the *Teal* for a voyage from Hertford to the Medway, the Colne, and other ports in the German and any other oceans, as the merchant shipping articles have it, I left Liverpool Street on the last day of July, with a kit-bag of portentous bulk and no slight weight, containing many changes of raiment, blankets, and a pair of sea-boots, bound for the station of Broxbourne, where I had been ordered to join the vessel. It seemed strange to be going inland with such an outfit, and most of my fellow passengers in the train thought I was just home from sea. The *Teal* had been spending the winter up country, and had been receiving sundry little additions to her comfort below deck, and when we turned out at four o'clock next morning she was looking as smart as paint and varnish could make her. A tug had been chartered and soon appeared, in the shape of a pony and a boy, and that kit-bag was soon bundled aboard, the tow rope was passed along, and we started. There was a slight difficulty in one of the locks, because the lock man, irritated, no doubt, at being hunted from his bed, refused to have anything to do with us until the dinghy had been paid for as a separate craft. There was nothing for it but to pay up and hope to recover at some future date, and to mock at the good man, and leave him gnashing his teeth at large by the side of his lock. Then came a stately progress through long and peaceful reaches and pretty country locks, until at last the sky in front of us grew smoky and the vegetation began to look grey and blighted, and the air was full of the perfumes of gas and manure works (and the river of defunct dogs), for we were getting near to London. At Clapton we discovered an ancient deep-keel yacht perched up on the bank, looking sadly out of place. It would have been a kindness if her owner had only broken her up, and, so to say, put her out of her misery years before; but that last kind office is seldom performed; and in all the harbours round the coast the poor old mouldering craft are left

123

to decay, a melancholy sight. There should be a marine undertaker's business combined with that of boat building, so that old craft might be taken away out of sight and broken up decently and reverently, instead of being left to lie about for years and years, showing all the ravages wrought by time and decay upon their poor anatomies. It is positively shocking, not to say indecent, to see them with bare ribs protruding here, stays hanging in shreds there, backs broken and so on, but there . . . I remember assisting in the removal of a poor old yacht from her berth at Chatham; it had to be done for fear lest she should sink at her moorings, and become hopelessly buried in the mud, a danger to navigation; and there was another old thing down there which had lain so long in one place uncared for, that when they tried to shift her, the keel fell bodily off.

At last, at Old Ford, we came to the last lock but one, a great big one, and beyond it was yawning a chasm of inky water, and we could hear the roar of town, and the tinkle of a tram car crossing a bridge, and we found ourselves among huge lighters, all on the move, and black walls of warehouses rose up from the water's edge, and we felt that the *Teal* would be like an eggshell if caught between some of those moving lighters. Our pony, too, was no longer of any use, and we struggled along as best we could, until getting into a tight place we found a friendly lighterman. "Better chuck us a line, sir; and come along astern of me. You'll be all right there, and we'll give you a pluck through the bridge. You won't get on any faster by yourselves. This is a funny place at tide time for a little craft, and there's a lot of lighters coming up now; we have to wait for them as we're going down." So we made ourselves as small as we could just under their stern, one of us at each end of the boat to fend her off, and glad we were of the shelter, for a procession of big fellows came hustling along on the flood, taking up all the room, and leaving none to spare. Then our turn came, and the friendly lighter moved ahead. It was a sight to see those two men handle their craft, and shove her along against the tide, and keep her straight and clear of the other lighters, and yet find time to sing and to chaff their neighbours, as though it were all child's play. "You'll get down to the lock just before high water, and go straight through

Brig at Anchor

while the gates are open," they told us; and soon we got to the lock, and they cast loose our tow-line, as they were not going through themselves, and giving us a final tug passed us on to the lock-man, who plucked us through in a moment, and we were out in Bow Creek. Here we waited to have a short spell and a second edition of lunch, and to say farewell to our pony; and then launched forth for further labour and toil, rowing and shoving along with the first of the ebb, but with a wind against us. We might have made sail with advantage, and saved a heap of time and trouble, by running out bowsprit, getting up the mast, and rigging her there; but as there were bridges further down, and we did not know quite what room we should have under them, we were afraid. It was a tiring and troublesome job against the wind, but at last the bridges were reached, and we were hailed cheerily from one of them, a swing bridge, which was open, and had the harbour-master (as we judged, from the excellence of his voice) perched at the end. "I wish I could see a tug, gentlemen, and I would give you a pluck down with pleasure. I wonder they did not give you a tow down from the lock; they ought to have seen you; but you'll soon be there now." And soon we could hear the clank of the iron shipbuilding yards, and see the masts of the tall Australian clippers in the East India Dock; and going alongside a lightship off the Trinity House Wharf, we set to work to rig the *Teal,* not forgetting to sound, for we had no time to spare, as the tide was ebbing fast. With great bustle we got rigged, and in a fatal moment, driven to it by fear of going aground, and not wishing to defile our new anchor with the mud of Bow Creek, we decided to start under jib and mizzen, and get the rest of the sail on her under way. Alas! for our brief career. Two minutes showed us our mistake, for there was a rushing ebb-tide outside, and Father Thames had us in the hollow of his hand; and, in a few moments, we drifted down on to a barge moored in the stream. No harm was done, luckily, and we made fast to her, and vowed not to start again till all sail was set, all ropes coiled down, and everything made shipshape; then giving her a trip up to windward she went clear of everything, and was off down the Thames. By this time we had been at it for twelve or fourteen hours, and were less eager for a long run down the river than we had been. On the contrary, each little bight we passed seemed to invite us to anchor. We remembered that there were usually some craft brought up just off the North Woolwich Gardens, and so we picked a berth there inside of some barges, and were very glad to finish our day by turning attention to the stowage of the cabin, which was nearly full of gear. Going in one at a time, the chaos was soon straightened out, supper discussed, riding-light hung up, and for a while we sat on deck in the light of the full moon, and watched the jolly old barges sliding along, and felt all the joy of being started on a summer cruise. But sleep was not to be denied, especially as there was to be another early start next day, and so 'twas "Go below, the Watch;" and, thanks to our friends the big barges moored outside, the night passed without alarms, even though the resting-place was not so peaceful and remote as the creeks and havens we hoped soon to be in possession of. Next morning found the active skipper abroad at four o'clock, and when he had brewed some tea and administered it to the torpid pilot, the latter began to feel ashamed of him-self, and turned out bravely, and soon the little *Teal* was off and away for her old haunts, rejoiced to have a nice south-westerly breeze to help her down. Quickly did the miles reel off, for she felt that she was leaving smoke and grime behind, and would soon again be at play with her old friends, the bil-lows of Sea Reach and the Swin. When passing Greenhithe each of us tried to teach the other the somewhat stale fact that Ingress Abbey was built of the stone of old London Bridge; but it was no go, we could only cast it at one another as a gibe. "Tell us something fresh, old man." Then we slipped past Gravesend, and I thought of the morning five or six years before when I had waited at the *Falcon* for the first appearance of the *Wild Rose*. Benson had been entrusted with the task of fetching her from Erith, and was to pick us up, and take us round to Chatham. What a day it was! What a joy to have a little craft of one's own! and how big the mainsail seemed, and what a length of boom (it was only fifteen feet long)! and what speed when a puff caught her! It was only afterwards, and by slow degrees, that one learnt that she was not quite perfection. Well, we passed Gravesend, stemming the flood in good style:

> *Until the forward creeping tides*
> *Began to foam, and we to draw*
> *From deep to deep, to where we saw*
> *The great ships lift their shining sides.*

And after passing the Ovens Buoy, as everything was going well, and not many vessels were about, we each in turn had a quiet snooze—first the pilot and then the skipper, and the breeze freshening with a bit of a squall now and then, when off Canvey Island, we kept her over to the southern shore, and, running close in out of the tide, had a good look at the entrance to the North Yantlet, and reckoned we should be at the mouth of the Medway a little before high water, and would be able to go in over everything. There were two or three barges going down the Jenkin Swatchway close in to the land, and we did the same, sounding from time to time just to make sure that the bottom of the river was in its right place, and by-and-bye we opened out the River Medway. "Now then, skipper, let her come up a bit more; we ain't going to run down to the Grain Edge Buoy this journey, but go overland, well inside the Martello; it's close on high-water time, and we ought to lie our course all the way from here into Stangate Creek."

"All right; get a pull of your sheets, and stand by to heave the lead, quartermaster."

"Aye, aye, sir."

Mainsheet and jib were soon in, and she was steering out of the Swatchway, and right over the top of the Grain Spit Sand, close in shore. No bottom, no bottom. "No sound, no ground, with a ten-foot pitch pine pole," by-and-bye the quartermaster sings out: "Touched, ten feet, ten feet, nine, nine, eight, eight, seven, seven, seven, keep her in, same, same, same, shoaling a little, shoaling a little, one fathom (by the deep, one), one fathom good, keep along like that, same, six feet, six, hard sand, hard sand, shoals a little, shoals. Hullo! stones that time, stones, now sand again. We must have crossed the causeway to the Martello; same water, deepens a little, deepens, we're over the top of it."

"Coil down the lead line, and keep her for Port Victoria. Here's Cockle-shell Hard; jolly place to land and sit in the sun, if we wanted to, but we'll do that s'mother day; and I can see Stangate Creek entrance, just off the end of the pier. We shall soon be home. There are some nice yachts off Port Victoria, and the *Wild Wave*, as usual; she's certain to be somewhere about. See her, that white yawl, or ketch rather. You know her owner, of course? There's the *Buccaneer*, too. Now run on, straight as you go, for that buoy; that's the entrance to Stangate. Ripping good passage we've made. The usual spit runs off across the mouth of the creek from the western side, but we shall have plenty of water to-day, and I'll get the anchor ready; we will bring up under the western shore. Would you like to run a long way up, or what?" "Well, Pilot, anything you like. You come aft, and take her where you think best. You know all about this place, I believe?" "Very well. We will bring up just beyond the first side creek—Sharfleet Creek, I think they call it, where the shore is fairly steep. Get your mizzen in, and then when you're forrard haul down the foresail." A few minutes more and she was edging in towards the western shore of Stangate.

OUR LADY OF CANVEY.

"All ready forrard?"

"All ready."

"I am just going to run her up into the wind."

Down went the helm and up she came, head to wind, moving slowly in towards the shore.

"Let go."

"All gone."

"Give her six fathoms''

"Aye, aye, sir," and in a twinkling the *Teal* was at anchor, sheltered nicely under the bank; sails stowed, and everything snug. The magnificent old creek full—ourselves the sole tenants, except a hulk moored near the mouth, and a bawley or two far away at the other end. So complete was our satisfaction at the good passage, that we promptly turned in to our bunks—it was only half-past two in the afternoon—and slept till five; then a bathe and supper, and a pipe, watching the *Teal* swinging softly to the ebb, and the anchor buoy bobbing like a fisherman's float just ahead of us. That anchor buoy was the new toy, elaborately made out of an old oil can, and painted in chequers, black and white; but alas, it had been jammed or trodden on, or something of the sort, which made it leaky, and on the following morning it was *non est*, having foundered in the night, and it was ignominiously fished up from the bottom, and surgically treated. After that it behaved better, but it was in disgrace.

Next day we were to potter about inside, so cameras were got ready; it turned out a perfect August day, and we revelled in the warmth and sunshine, rejoicing to be away in the wilds. After breakfast and a swim we trimmed up the *Teal* and took her portrait, and then started off in the dinghy, and rowed into Sharfleet Creek, and were surprised at its size and its great lonely bights and headlands, with a little farmhouse here and there nestling on the shore, and with room for any number of yachts; then rounding a point we came into another reach, with an old oyster watch boat moored in the middle; so we went and parleyed with the watchman and gave him tobacco, and asked him all sorts of questions.

Did he think we could get through and out at the other end?

"Oh, yes. You go right along; there's another oyster boat further on, and plenty of water, and near her you can get out at high-water time into Long Reach; they will tell you where the passage is."

"Good; I vote we try it to-morrow, and go up to Chatham that way; but I think we ought to go to Halstow this afternoon, it's worth doing."

"All right, let's set the lug sail now and get back to the Teal," which we did, and made sail and went up to Halstow, and made fast to an old mooring buoy near the primitive wharf. The place was just simmering in the heat, and we went ashore to try and find some dinner. There was an inn there kept by an old man-of-war's man, who had given us dinner once before when we were in those parts, and we tried hard to find his house, but could not. We found

Above Bridge, Rochester

another excellent inn, though, and absorbed much shandy gaff, and had good
roast beef for ninepence apiece, and took photographs, and looked about us,
and then went back to the *Teal,* for the tide is not at Halstow very long. By the
way, the rules of the local cricket club, as posted up in the inn parlour, were
very fine—here are some of them:

"That any member making a false accusation against another shall be
fined twopence."

"That any member leaving the Club shall forfeit all subscriptions."

"That no fresh rules be made during the present year."

The other rules were also most excellent; the fine for bad language we
noted was—one penny.

Our first act on getting back to the *Teal* was to shake off most of our shore-
clothes, for the heat was tremendous, and slowly we drifted down again,
and brought up in our old berth for a quiet night, taking final snap-shots at
the sunset after supper-time. Next day, we were under way at first-quarter
flood, and boldly pushed the *Teal* into Sharfleet Creek, and sailed on till watch
vessel number two was reached. There we saw the outlet into the river, so
steered into it till we ran aground, and then went out in the dinghy to explore
and sound for the channel. There was plenty of water at half-flood, except for
a causeway of stones at one place, so we brought the *Teal* down to that, and
waited, because it was nearly dead calm, and the tide might begin to come in
against us, and give us trouble. After rowing to the watch vessel, and chatting
with the people on board, we came back to the *Teal,* and soon we had water
over the stones, and emerged into Half Acre Creek, at its junction with Long
Reach, and began to wonder how we were to reach Chatham, as the wind was
gone, the heat of the sun having "eaten it all up." Still, the tide would flow for
a couple of hours, or more, and the end of it was that we got to Upnor just as
the tide turned, and then tried to row her along. After frantic exertions, we
squeezed her up to Upnor Castle, and anchored near the end of the causeway,
a very convenient and safe berth, better in many respects than if we had gone
on to Chatham. We decided to keep her there, and to use the dinghy for going
to the towns in; and as we were beginning to pine for civilisation, we promptly

put on shore-clothes and went in search of it, leaving a trusty boy in charge, with orders to hang up the riding-light when it got dark.

We spent the evening pleasantly on shore, and came back to the *Teal* laden with stores, fruit and newspapers, to find the riding-light up and the *Teal* all safe, and we made another journey to Rochester next day, and took photographs, and looked at places for anchoring in, and rummaged in old book shops, and nearly succeeded in securing some jolly long French rolls to take back with us, but not quite, for they had all been eaten up when we called for them, so we had to be content with bread of the ordinary shape, and finally said good-bye, and went off to Queenborough in the evening, after taking a final walk round Upnor, to try and pick the most convenient berth, in case we should want to come again and stay there for a few days.

CHAPTER XI

To Woodbridge ~ Bawdsey Haven ~ The River Deben

"WELL, THIS IS DISGRACEFUL; after all our good resolutions, too! We don't deserve to carry any flood into Bawdsey Haven, and there is not much chance of getting in over the ebb if this wind holds. Take another swig on those jib-halliards, and then coil down."

The skipper was wroth, for we were clearing out of Brightlingsea Creek at ten o'clock in the day, instead of between five and six, as we had solemnly vowed to do overnight, and the vessels anchored in the Colne were already beginning to swing to the young flood. Yet a landsman might have found some excuse for us, for we had had a high old dusting the previous day, with no food to speak of until nightfall; beating down to the Colne from Harty Ferry, at the back of the Isle of Sheppey, under reefed mainsail and small jib, with the wind heading us to the last, and spitefully drawing off the land as soon as we were through the Wallet Spitway. It was almost due north now, and the *Teal* was cracking on for the Bar Buoy with all she could carry, to make up for those Morpheus stolen hours.

"Yes, it's pretty bad; but this breeze will take us over the tide, if it holds—and it isn't half a bad day. Let me get some breakfast under weigh; when I have filled you up with eggs and bacon—bacon is the tack in a sea way, it doesn't spill in the cooking—you won't have a pain in your mind. No, don't haul her up yet awhile, better keep right on to the buoy, and then lay a course over the Priory Spit for the end of Clacton Pier; there'll be water for us over the Collier by the time we get there, and we don't want to get hung on these 'black hills' now, as we shall do if we cut it too fine round Colne Point. Where's the mustard tin? Oh! all right. Now for the little stove. Keep her as steady as you can, if you love your coffee."

So the Pilot, Cook and Joint-sailing-master braced himself against the starboard bunk, raised a cloud of grateful culinary incense so powerful that it travelled up the wind into the helmsman's nostrils, as the latter put the helm down, and hauled his wind outside the old red buoy. Then the Pilot jumped forward and set up the peak; and jumped aft again even more quickly, just in time to save his bacon from decorating the cabin floor. That bacon did not have much further chance of travelling about on its own account, and when its accompanying eggs and coffee had been safely stowed away, and the subsequent pipes were in full blast, we were passing Clacton, and life certainly began to seem less discouraging. There was a smart breeze still; and keeping close in to cheat the tide, we were doing very well through the smoother water under an off-shore wind. The holiday makers bunched on the pier-head in the usual fashion as we passed under them, and no doubt made the usual remarks on the folly and general imbecility of the two idiots who pretended to find pleasure in working by themselves, amid dirt and salt-water, on a little boat. We also made remarks, and one or two of the down-gazing faces were worth remarking; at least the Pilot-Bard (he is a poet by constitution) said that the pink lining of a parasol gave an additional charm to her lovely complexion, and then proceeded to a further investigation of the chromatic problem with the aid of the ship's glass. The skipper discourages this sort of thing as a rule, but is always ready to make allowance for the amiable weaknesses of others.

The tide had more heart in it, and it seemed a long time before we were off Walton Pier, and in full view of the crowded cars which were rushing up and down their new switchback railway.

Quoth the pilot, "The man who invented the switchback has taken the measure of humanity; it is essentially a combination of undulation and vibration, with giddiness thrown in; and you end a little lower than you began. I should say—"

"My good friend, if you have leisure to moralize on life, you can take the tiller for a bit. From my point of view life is nothing, if not practical and well-regulated. The altitude of the sun suggests cheese and beer. There's no reason, because breakfast was late, to postpone luncheon; we should soon lose a whole day's meals at that rate; have some? That's better. Hand those moral reflections over to your brother for his next sermon, and let the trippers alone to enjoy themselves. No good keeping her close in any longer; the hard ground shoals out a long way hereabouts. Steer just inside the red and white buoy in the Medusa Channel, and then head for Landguard Point; we shall steal a little flood that way."

So we stood across the estuary, out of which a little tug was towing a big full-rigged ship in ballast, so light that she rolled broad streaks of copper out of the green swell, and we watched the cloud-shadows drift over the glacis of the forts, and fetched out cameras, and made a shot at the bell-buoy, and missed it; and decided that some day we would really explore the Stour, and go up to Wrabness and see what sort of a berth was to be found up there among the mud flats, in the channel which is so tortuous that the bargees say it must have been made by an eel. We just shaved Landguard Point, and kept in as near as possible to the extremities of the abominable Felixstowe groins, and chuckled to find that, by so doing, we could give the go-by to a coasting schooner which had picked us up off Clacton. The wind had drawn more from the nor'ard again, and the old coaster was soaking to leeward like a barrel. Presently, he put his helm down, spilling the wind out of his head sails, leisurely clewed up his top-sail, hauled down fore stay-sail, and triced up his main tack.

"The old man doesn't like being beaten, and doesn't mean to chafe his gear this tide. Turn in, all hands, the old woman will take the watch. Shall we run out to him, and offer him a pluck down?"

"There is Felixstowe Church, and the big new house they have just finished building, with a wall all round it, as if they expected another deluge. And there, beyond, is the southernmost of the two Martello Towers; they are the other side of the entrance to the haven. Stand out a little when you are off that first tower, and make for the buoy in the channel, or you may get hung up on the spit, which sometimes runs out a long way. There is lots of water for us now, probably, but these banks and knolls shift in the most various fashions with the winter storms, and it never does to trust to one's recollection of what the entrance was like last year; and as to charts, they are an absolute delusion. That will do. "Now then, pinch her all you can; we have got the ingoing flood with us; and I will get the pole overboard to starboard.

There is the top of the big knoll just awash. At low water it is all dry beach right up to the cliffs. We sailed in over the beach from Aldeburgh once in the early morning, and found a leveret imprisoned on the knoll by the rising tide. What could have taken him there overnight, goodness only knows! Keep her just full, now; no bottom; the same; touched; seven foot. Keep her full, and stand by to go about; seven; six; six and a half; five—ready about! 'Bout she goes! Now you can stand right in to the western shore; the shingle bank is steep-to. There is a man—there always is at least one man—digging potatoes. Shall we land and get some?" "All right." "Give her another trip across then, and we will bring up just round the point yonder, where you see the masts of that old dismantled brig." So we gave her a couple of trips in, the wind falling light as we neared the shore, and then "Ready the anchor forrard ! Shake her, so! Now fore-sheet aweather; that will do, let go, down sail; that's all right; now we will just get a lashing round the mainsail, and then give all hands shore leave."

Pulling the dinghy up on to the shingle, we make her painter fast to a casual anchor lying there, and stroll across the dene-like waste, to where a coast-guardsman off duty is forking the spuds out of his sand-patch. He sells us half a bucketful readily enough, and, after a few minutes' gossip, we make for the boat again in company with old Newson, the local pilot, who is bringing down from his shed some renovated gear for his boat, which is lying in the little bay where we landed. She is a beamy sloop, decked in over the fore-sheets only, with a floor flat and broad as a ball-room, ballasted with a couple of fish trunks filled with shingle placed just aft of her mast. Just the craft though, as one of us knows, for lifting one dry over the heavy tumbling seas which a north-easter brings crowding into the haven. "Oh, yes, she's a rare stiff old thing."

Newson says: "You've got a new ship, sir, I see; an useful looking one too, and more comfortable than the other you used to have, I dare say. No, I wouldn't change with ye; we want plenty of room for our fishing work, and we don't have no use for no cabins. Are you going to stop here? "

"No," we tell him, "we are going up to Woodbridge."

"Well, you won't get there by daylight; that'll be high flood in less than an hour, and the wind's dead against ye all the way, and falling light, too. That'll go to the west'ard, though, by sunset."

We will see what can be done, anyway; so we pull on board again, make sail, and get up the mudhook, and work by short boards past the half-mile long island of sand and shingle, which lies right in the middle of the river below King's Fleet. Then we have rather easier times, for at this state of the tide we can stand well over the mud banks to either shore; we keep the pole going whenever we get inside the beacon line, but the water is so clear that one can see the weedy bottom easily, and we don't fear being hung up—we are carrying no tide, however, by the time we make Ramsholt Dock; and as we open its relatively spacious bay, with two trim yachts and a dozen other small craft moored within the shelter of its pier and cliff-like shore, the Bard proposes that we should bring up, and explore the country. "Doesn't look half a bad place for a house—and you can keep your boat in the puddle at your front door," he says. We pick a convenient berth, stow the sails, and make things ship-shape; refill our tobacco pouches and match-boxes, and presently paddle ashore. We climb the heights near the old church, with its few wind-bent trees, and on the level top we find a pleasant breeze to temper the hot sun. Beyond Hollesley Church to the eastward, we catch glimpses of the lower reaches of the Alde and of Orford, with its ruinous church and castle, nestling amid trees. To the south lies the North Sea, blue, breezy and sparkling, and in the north-western distance a patch of cloud-like smoke marks the whereabouts of Ipswich. Other churches, Shottisham, Boyton and Bawdsey, dot the level; and here and there sparse rows of tall trees, bent and scant of foliage for the most part, tell of the gales which often sweep inland from the sea. We sat down amongst the long dry grass under the lee of a little bank, and lazily discussed the *pros* and *cons* of a country house in this region to a chorus of grasshoppers and bumble-bees till late in the afternoon. Then we walked down to the pier, and bought some fresh eggs from the landlady at the little public-house, where the Bard gathered valuable information as to the local landowners while sampling the Woodbridge ale. It was half ebb when we got

Sunset

on board again, but the water alongside was quite salt enough to boil the potatoes properly, and by our united efforts we elaborated a really *recherché* dinner.
It was a hot, clear night, and we sat out in the well until long after the tide had
turned. Earlier in the day someone had made the suggestion of sailing up by
moonlight. But there was no wind to speak of, and that project was tacitly
ignored as we lay in the shadow of the point watching the moonshine grow
and brighten along the stream beyond, while the stars paled overhead. One by
one the few lights on shore were extinguished. Strange sounds floated rarely
and at longer intervals over the water, softened like the ghosts of a day's activ-
ity. We could hear the tide creeping over the mudbanks, and now and again
the croak and flop of an alighting heron. A peewit cried plaintively from the
marshes on the other side of the stream; and an owl somewhere up by the old
church was hooting at our intrusive riding light in a disparaging manner. Low
in the sky to the northward glowed the ruddy flames of the cement works at
Waldringfield. All the bustle of human life had been shut down, and we were
alone amid a million ripples whispering in the moonlight.

We had a swim in the slack water before breakfast, and got under weigh
with a gentle breeze from west-northwest, which kindly freshened on the
flood, so that the ship was able to lie up almost every reach. There was plenty
of mud visible now, especially above Shottisham; and in places the herons
covered it in regiments, like sparrows on a wheat stack. But the channel is
well marked by plenty of stout beacons, and its edge is fairly steep-to, in all
the lower reaches, so that it is easy to avoid getting the shore aboard, per-
manently, at all events. We touched for a few minutes at "Troublesome Corner," which well deserves its title, but the flowing tide promptly set us free;
and then, with the breeze lighter and more puffy under the heights, we crept
on for another half-mile or so, and brought up just below Woodbridge Quay.
There we landed, and bought some papers at the railway station, and were
pleased to find that the world at large had not seriously gone wrong since our
directing influence had been withdrawn from the management of its affairs.
Then we climbed into the town and did some marketing—in fruit mainly—
and the skipper made his usual purchase of a teacup and saucer, inscribed

"A Present from Woodbridge," to add to that collection of crockery which he calls his cruising memorial set. He says it is to be handed down in his family as an heirloom for generations. And his friends have remarked with surprise on the exceptional modesty, or truthfulness, which has hitherto prevented his buying anything that displays the frequent legend, "For a Good Boy." We seized the opportunity of celebrating some other fellow's birthday by the unusual extravagance of an hotel lunch, for which orgie the Bard always declares there must be ample warrant in the well-known statement of Tennyson cum Babbage:

Every minute dies a man,
And one and one-sixteenth is born.

Afterwards we rowed across to the ferry landing-place, and the skipper initiated his companion into the exact position from which to evoke the fine quadruple echo, and made him prove its existence by a polysyllabic and hair-curling Cymric war-shout, which brought all the workmen tumbling out from a big warehouse on the quay, in horror and dismay. After that it seemed better to take advantage of a fair wind down on the ebb. The Deben is navigable for a few miles above Woodbridge, but the stream is narrow, and the banks flat and uninteresting; so that we did not hanker after further wanderings in that direction. "What do they make here?" queried the Bard, giving a last look round as we tumbled on board, and began to make sail.

"Beer, I believe, mainly. But Fitz-Gerald, who had a house here, proposed to name one of his boats the *Scandal*, on the ground that this was the 'Staple of Woodbridge.' It is not a very saleable commodity, I should think, though, except in the form of a society paper."

We negotiated Troublesome Point all right this time, and ran down stream with a flowing sheet, and a wind that followed free. The flood had ousted all the herons from their mudflats, and only an occasional gull, and flocks of restless ox-birds, swayed and flitted along the banks of a broad sheet of water blinking in the sunshine. Off the quay at Waldringfield a little schooner was lying; she must have come up with the last flood for a cargo of cement; another job for old Newson. We ran on past Ramsholt with some reluctance, and brought up in the little bight below the island, intending to get out with the ebb early next morning, and to make a long day up into the Thames. After dinner we went ashore; the wind was from the north again now, and dark moist-looking wisps of vapour were drawn across the sombre glow of a dull sun-set; the glass was going down, too. "Sea-boots again to-morrow, old man! But we have had a jolly trip, so far, and we shan't mind some wet, if only the wind will bustle us up to town in time." We prowled down towards the Martello Towers, and ran against two of the ever-civil Coastguard fraternity in the chill gloaming. Of course there was plenty to talk of, and they gave us some useful hints as to the present lie of the bar, and about the best way of getting out on the ebb. One of the men had served on board the *Danae*, on the West Coast of Africa, and was a regular walking children's book about the ship's pets, the dogs and the monkeys, and especially the twin goats, one of which, adopted by the quarter-deck, grew so haughty that he would never let his brother come aft the mainmast, though he, probably, did not have such good times as "Billy," in the forecastle; and of the cat, which had been saved from three sinking ships, including the unlucky *Vanguard*; and, lastly, of his own special pet, a small grey parrot, with feathers that stuck out "all ways," like a Friesland fowl; who was an accomplished linguist, and whose only fault was the ineradicable habit of pecking and chipping the whitewash from the forecastle deck beams; of how its owner was always ready to repair damages by laying on a fresh coat of whitewash himself; of how one day, at last, the boatswain declared that the bird was a blank nuisance, beyond all hope of redemption, and further stated that if he found it guilty of the same practices hereafter, he would strangle it forthwith, and chuck it overboard; of how its master, like a modern maritime Virginius, replied that that should never be; and how, thereupon striding to the spot where his parrot was innocently swinging on a ringbolt, he twisted its neck with one swift, painless wrench, and then—"laid his head down on the table, and sobbed like a baby;" the tears even now trembling in his voice at the recital.

There was a dark bank to windward, and ragged wisps of cloud were speeding across a watery moon when we turned in; and the ripples under the bows slapped the planking with the sharp metallic sound that bodes a rising breeze.

The next morning was one of driving rain-squalls from the north and north-east. We got out early, at about half-ebb, through the short surf tumbling on the bar, and fitted the dinghy with a second painter, as a preventer in case of accidents, and the ship settled down for her journey home. How the old girl did bustle! There was not much to do except jam your foot up against the lee coaming of the well, and get the other man to light a pipe for you inside the cabin now and then, and pray that no gear should carry away; but the Bard found time to blow a kiss towards Clacton, as we sped past its dripping and deserted pier. We carried the flood right up to Leigh, where we doffed our oileys, at the conclusion of one of the best runs we had ever made in the good little boat, and handed her over to the care of Benson, to lie at rest upon the mud opposite the Coastguard until the time should come for another long trip down Swin to Harwich, or perhaps to Lowestoft.

And here this history must come to a close. It would perhaps have been more complete if we could have given an account of a cruise to Harwich, and a trip up the Stour, and by the Orwell to Ipswich, for the latter river ought not to be missed, and Pin Mill, about half-way up, is a sweet place for a night's anchorage. But our cruises to Harwich have been for the most part uneventful; and when one has got down into the Wallet, the rest of the way is rather uninteresting, particularly when there is a fair wind and plenty of daylight; and the run from the Thames to Harwich is too far for a small boat to try, except under such favourable conditions.

In Harwich harbour the anchorage for small boats is not very good, and the space is rather taken up by local craft.

Most of the smaller vessels bring up just off the town, or squeeze into the basins if they can find room. A little higher up there is anchorage ground close to the mud, but it must be to the southward of the line of buoys which mark the track left clear for the mail boats. Or one can cross over to the Shotley side and bring up under the point of land, choosing the Stour or the Orwell, according to the direction of the wind. It is very quiet and nice over there, but rather a long way from the town and the shops.

And now, friendly reader, farewell, or at least *au revoir*, until perchance our little boats may meet in some lone creek, or cruise together down Swin, through Swale or Swatchway.

A NOTE ON THE PHOTOGRAPHS

We are fortunate that the photographs printed in the original edition of *Swin, Swale & Swatchway* were not half-tone screened (as re-screening generally results in quality problems) but instead reproduced by an unidentified continuous tone process. In both the original and current editions of the book they are printed at negative size, and so appear fairly sharp. The slight mottling visible in them is due to the heavily textured original paper surface, an effect which could not be removed in the current reproductions without losing tonal information in the images. All but three of the photos were taken on the Eclipse folding hand camera, of mahogany construction, manufactured by Shew of London in the 1880s and 90s. It employs glass plates giving a negative size 3¼ by 4¼ inches. The publishers are grateful to Mr. Rob Tooley for supplying the above photograph.